D0466406

EAT LIKE A GILMORE

The Unofficial
Cookbook for Fans
of Gilmore Girls
by
KRISTI CARLSON

Photography by Bonnie Matthews

Skyhorse Publishing

Copyright © 2016 by Kristi Carlson

All rights reserved. No part of this publication may be reproduced or stored in a retrieval system or transmitted in any form or by any means, whether electronic, mechanical photocopying, recording or other kind, without the prior permission in writing of the owners.

All inquiries should be addressed to Skyhorse Publishing, 307 West 36th Street, 11th Floor, New York, NY 10018.

Skyhorse Publishing books may be purchased in bulk at special discounts for sales promotion, corporate gifts, fund-raising, or educational purposes. Special editions can also be created to specifications. For details, contact the Special Sales Department, Skyhorse Publishing, 307 West 36th Street, 11th Floor, New York, NY 10018 or info@skyhorsepublishing.com.

Skyhorse® and Skyhorse Publishing® are registered trademarks of Skyhorse Publishing, Inc.®, a Delaware corporation.

Visit our website at www.skyhorsepublishing.com.

10 9 8 7

Names: Carlson, Kristi, author. | Matthews, Bonnie, 1963- photographer
   (expression)
Title: Eat like a Gilmore : the unofficial cookbook for fans of Gilmore girls
   / by Kristi Carlson ; photography by Bonnie Matthews.
Description: New York : Skyhorse Publishing, [2016]
Identifiers: LCCN 2016038186| ISBN 9781510717343 (hardback) | ISBN
   9781510717350 (eBook)
Subjects: LCSH: Cooking. | Food in popular culture. | Food on television. |
   Gilmore girls (Television program) | BISAC: COOKING / Entertaining. |
   LCGFT: Cookbooks.
Classification: LCC TX714 .C37336 2016 | DDC 641.5--dc23 LC record available at
   https://lccn.loc.gov/2016038186

Cover design by Brian Anderson
Cover photos by Bonnie Matthews, except author photo by Jay Andrino, Lightzone Photography
All recipe photos by Bonnie Matthews, except page 93 by iStockphoto/ALLEKO

ISBN: 978-1-5107-1734-3
eBook ISBN: 978-1-5107-1735-0

Printed in the United States of America

This book is unofficial and unauthorized. It is not authorized, approved, licensed, or endorsed by Warner Bros. Entertainment, Inc. Trademarks used in this book are property of their respective owners and are used for informational purposes only.

Dedication

To my grandmother, Lottie, with love and gratitude, for her patient,
gentle guidance, both in and out of the kitchen.

To Amy Sherman-Palladino, with respect and gratitude, for introducing
me to unique, confident, female role-models.

CONTENTS

456

Author's Note

789

KRISTI CARLSON

As a *Gilmore Girls* fan since the original Tuesday night airing of Season 1 back in 2000, I've taken a lot of ribbing over the years. Back before it became "cool" to watch and love *Gilmore Girls*, it was kind of the nerdy, cat lady thing to watch. I didn't care. The Donna Reed episode was the first one I watched, and I was hooked. About the time the Chilton bake sale came along, I was on full food alert, too, wanting to try everything. Since then—seriously, for fifteen years—I've been patiently waiting for a cookbook so I could try all of the Gilmore foods. Summer 2015 is when my patience finally gave way. I decided to just figure them out myself. That one thought lead to this cookbook.

This project combines two of my great loves: cooking and *Gilmore Girls*. It's given me the opportunity to meet so many positive, fun fellow fans—people who speak the special Gilmore language. I mean, I've been able to sign off my emails with "YA-YA!" or "HUZZAH!" and have people write back talking about Anaglypta® wallpaper. To feel understood like that—it's been soul-soothing.

One thing I really didn't expect from this project is how many of the contributors would be from my home state of Michigan. Michigan is the home of my childhood, where I spent summers visiting my grandparents, and it's the place where my grandma first taught me to cook and bake. The sounds and smells, foods, seasons, and traditions of Michigan make up much of who I am. After living in Southern California for more than thirty years, Michigan often feels very far away. So this opportunity to work with several of my fellow stateswomen has brought the Michigan girl buried somewhere in me back out. That's a good thing. She's a much sweeter version of me.

Not to say that I don't love living in California—I do! I live in Burbank with my boyfriend, Tim, about three blocks from the Warner Brothers main lot where *Gilmore Girls* is filmed. We're one block from the Warner Ranch, where the Dragonfly Inn is located. During the original series, my proximity to the studios provided some pretty incredible opportunities. For example, I once got invited to visit the set. I went, of course. I sat in one of those folding director's chairs next to the line producer, only one person away from Scott Patterson. We were seated on the edge of Luke's Diner, watching Lauren Graham as she was being filmed. I don't remember much about that experience, other than I managed not to geek out on any of the cast members—a major success.

Here I am, more than a decade later, more of a fan than ever. I'm happy I finally found both a way to turn my fanaticism into something tangible and something that would connect me with other fans. Boy, has it! After a few months of noodling around in the kitchen, testing the feasibility of this cookbook, I embarked on a simple Kickstarter campaign hoping to find a few like-minded fans of both the show and the food. Literally, overnight, the campaign turned into a whirlwind of press and pledges, which helped me raise far more money than I originally needed. In addition to money, I was getting so many notes from people: people eager for me to include their favorite recipe, thrilled to be able to order a *Gilmore Girls* cookbook, and grateful to me for taking this on. It has all felt surreal and has filled my heart with a ton of love. I've found my people!

Along the way, I had the good fortune to be approached by Skyhorse Publishing – by two fellow *Gilmore Girls* fans from their cookbook team. They wanted to get involved. I was thrilled to have the support of a fast-growing, small publisher. They have everything I don't: the experience of publishing a slew of great cookbooks, access to the best book printers and binders, and talented sales and PR teams. The moment Skyhorse and I struck a deal, this book became ten times better. Our partnership allowed for more recipes, higher quality photographs, better paper and binding – basically more and better everything!

Of course, writing about this process in a couple of paragraphs makes it seem far quicker and easier than it was. Just like Lorelai and Sookie opening the Dragonfly, I experienced many "sugarfoot!" moments. The only way I've gotten through many of them is with the help (and sanity) of others. So while it may be just my name and Bonnie's on the cover, there've been many, many people behind the scenes helping out. In particular, I'd like to thank one person – Tim Kelly – for being script supervisor, tote board updater, head taster, head dishwasher, grocery store runner, photo model, photo assistant, prop master, driver, launderer, cheerleader, and psychotherapist. He was also the person who originally gave me the idea to make this book. Tim has lived in the midst of all the chaos and stuff that has taken over our home, and he hasn't complained even one time. He's my Luke. My Richard. My Jackson. My penguin.

If it weren't for his help and support, this cookbook would not exist. Period.

Now that you know how the book was made, let's talk about the book itself. The first thing I had to do was make several decisions, like which recipes to include, how to attribute each recipe to the character who originally made it, and how to organize the recipes into a usable format.

One of the first things I had to figure out was how to address the food Lorelai and Rory eat at home. How would I incorporate the Chinese takeout, the Pop-Tarts®, the spray cheese, and the pizza? Right away the answer was obvious: I wouldn't. I mean, I couldn't. There's just no recreating a delivery pizza. Or a Moroccan grab bag from Al's. Each one is a specialty, an art unto itself. Many have tried to replicate these foods at home. Many have failed. To eat the way Lorelai and Rory eat at home, all you need is a drawer full of takeout menus, a magnet on the fridge with the number for the pizza place, and a convenience store down the street. You don't need a cookbook.

Next came choosing the recipes I *would* include, which was the easiest task of all. I searched my own memory banks for the dishes I'd been clamoring to try for over a decade. Then people who pledged to the campaign wrote and told me the recipes they wanted to see. Finally, I perused episodes to search for hidden gems to help round out the list. What you have in your hands is a book of recipes for over 100 dishes—each of them eaten, served, or mentioned on the show. Of course, it doesn't include *every* dish from the show; it would take a book two or three times the size of this one to fully cover everything! So if there is a dish that is very important to you that you don't see inside, drop me a note. I'll see what I can do.

Once the recipes were chosen, next step was attributing them to their maker. You'll notice each recipe has a little icon on the page indicating the recipe is from Luke's Diner, Sookie's Kitchen, Emily's House, or is a Town Favorite. In addition, the recipe is written in a style that suits its maker. Luke's recipes can be made quickly and pretty easily, and they include a few shortcuts, like canned sauce or jarred gravy. This is designed to mimic cooking at the diner. Emily's recipes use only the finest ingredients—and some of the ingredients are difficult to find. For instance, the squab will likely have to be purchased from a butcher specializing in poultry and game. Sookie's recipes are from scratch, period. Many of them are very detailed and require several steps. There are no shortcuts to making her dishes. For Town Favorites, because they encompass everything from Miss Patty's Founders Day Punch to Logan's Paella, anything goes!

Finally, I chose to write the recipes assuming readers would have few small appliances. I wanted to encourage people to cook, not turn them off by requiring too many expensive machines. So you won't see a recipe demanding a stand mixer or a deep fryer or even a microwave. Nearly every recipe in this book can be made using basic appliances like a stove, oven, hand mixer, a Dutch oven, and a bunch of inexpensive utensils and gadgets. If you have the fancier stuff – terrific! Use anything you've got. A handful of recipes do demand specialty equipment, like ice cream. Yes, ice cream can be made without an ice cream maker. I've tried it – with the rock salt, the ice, the shaking, and the mess. It's not worth it. Go buy ice cream for five bucks. If you're determined to make ice cream at home, invest in a $50 ice cream maker.

As for ingredients, I used the same philosophy, keeping the ingredients as simple as possible. Flour is flour. Sugar is sugar. Butter is butter. In the few instances where a recipe calls for Cake Flour or Superfine Sugar, or Unsalted Butter – rest assured, it's written that way because using the specific ingredient improved the quality of the dish. For the vast majority of recipes, regular ol' ingredients will work just fine. In the Reference Guide, all of the assumptions, abbreviations, and suggested gadgets are listed. So be sure to check out those pages before you jump into trying the first recipe.

Finally, I'd like to say "thank you" to the 1,244 people who made this book possible by pledging their personal money to the Kickstarter campaign. They trusted an unproven, first-time author, and for that, I'm immensely grateful. In addition to money, a few of them contributed their time and their culinary expertise – the feature writers, boosters, recipe contributors, and recipe testers who added so much good juju to this project. You'll get to meet them in a few pages. They are super fans of either the show, or of me, or both. I'm so happy I've had this opportunity to work with all of them.

I'd like to send out thanks to all of these amazing folks, as well:

Brian Anderson of Anderson Design for his beautiful work designing every page of this book

Abigail Gehring, Chamois Holschuh, Sam Levitz, and Jaidree Braddix at Skyhorse for partnering with me and sharing their expertise

Bonnie Matthews for sharing her cookbook expertise and for taking such beautiful photos

Oxana Shabunov for styling each photo and keeping cool under pressure

Krista Haitz for directing and filming the Kickstarter video

Vianna Vigneau for assisting with the Kickstarter video

Rene Rodriguez for making my hair and make-up look good

Jonathan Kirsch for representing me

Jay Andrino of Lightzone Photography for taking the cover photo of me

Krystie Lee Yandoli for taking the time to write the article that set off a press storm

Thomas at Puritan Pride for finding me turkeys in the middle of May

Jose and his team at Make Easy Maids for keeping my kitchen from becoming a salmonella laboratory

Handy Market and the Instacart app for getting all of the ingredients to me

The Kickstarter Team for selecting this project as a "Project We Love"

Jenny Whitaker of Kindred Handicrafts for her pep talks

Lynn Tomei Schlundt for her friendship and for always supporting my projects—even the wacky ones

The Cordovians for taking all the leftovers and for bringing me cocktails when I needed them most

Ultimately, this book is for you: the fans. I hope these recipes help make Stars Hollow a bit more tangible in your life, by bringing its food into your home.

There will never be another show like *Gilmore Girls*.

Copper Boom!

Kristi

MY LITTLE CORNER OF THE WORLD

My name is Marisa, but artistically and on the interwebs, I go by **Ember Quillweb**. I'm a fast talkin', coffee guzzlin', artsy kinda gal, who has many parallels to the *Gilmore Girls*. I'm kind of a Jill of all trades, but mainly I make art, craft, and I really love doing interior and small scale exterior garden design, as well as staging. I have a large animal family, and I am a collector of old things and old books (I actually had a birthday party trip to Mark Twain's house in Hartford, Connecticut, and yes, I coincidentally have a magnet of his head on my fridge). I also have an affinity for secondhand clothes that started as a child; I love coming up with themes for clothes, as well as wearing turn of the century dresses when I have to do the dishes.

My love for *Gilmore Girls* started the moment I saw the promo commercial many moons ago; I can recall thinking "I must watch this show." Since the night *Gilmore Girls* premiered, I haven't stopped watching (thank you DVD box sets—I'm on my third set). Sometimes, I think my sheer willpower and devotion to watching—as if the show never ended—helped bring it back. *Gilmore Girls* makes me feel good, it's helped me through tough times, and the show itself has been the Gilmore I wish I knew and could be. And now it's back, and I am not surprised. It was never over for me.

Anyhow, I always wanted to expand my love of the show into something that I do, and I finally have. I have taken my love of collecting and reselling vintage clothes and melded it with the fashion of the show, to open an online secondhand shop devoted to clothing inspired by the show. I even offer pieces seen on the show.

Getting a *Gilmore Girls* clothing collection together has been a lot of work, but a lot of fun—especially making the little Stars Hollow sets I use as the backdrop for photographs of the clothing. Just consider me your *Gilmore Girls* personal stylist: I will help you navigate through the rhinestone-studded shirts on your way to some great, timeless pieces!

One of my dream jobs, of course, would be to have some part in one of Amy's worlds—I am for hire! So, go make yourself a Cup o' Luke's, and come visit one of my online realms.

For my *Gilmore Girls* clothing shop:
Website: **GilmoreGarbs.com**
Facebook: **www.facebook.com/GilmoreGarbs**
Instagram: **www.instagram.com/GilmoreGarbs**

For my artistic endeavors:
Facebook: **www.facebook.com/TheCraftyFoxPage**
Instagram: **www.instagram.com/ember_quillweb**
Etsy: **etsy.com/shop/TheWoodlandWardrobe**

I also have a Facebook page just for fun ranting of all things Gilmore:
www.facebook.com/GilmoreGirlsUniteAndEatPie

For all other inquires, like if you want me to barista your dog's Bark Mitzvah, or Gilmorize your living quarters, even Babette-gnome-bomb your garden, you can reach me here: **e.quillweb@gmail.com**

CAKEAPOTAMUS

My name is **Mandi Buckalew**, and I own **Cakeapotamus**, a custom, small-batch bakery and cake studio in Opelika, Alabama. I live in Opelika, a small town about ninety minutes south of Atlanta, with my husband and two kids. When we were dating, my husband and I used to watch reruns of *Gilmore Girls*. Even after twelve years of marriage, we still watch *Gilmore Girls* on Netflix.

Cakeapotamus is nothing like Weston's Bakery in Stars Hollow. We're far less traditional, and my bakery is decorated with my collection of geeky memorabilia rather than the usual bakery flowers and hearts. As much as I would like to be like Fran or Sookie, I actually identify pretty strongly with Lorelai. I talk too fast, drink lots of coffee, and make bad jokes. I make up bits and somehow get people to join me in crazy schemes. Oh, and I have a Hello Kitty toaster. I even put myself through business school at night at the local community college to learn how to run my own business—an idea I got from *Gilmore Girls*.

My journey to owning the bakery has been an interesting one. Before I opened the bakery, I was a teacher for adolescents with behavior problems. My master's degree is actually in special education. Before that, I studied animal behavior and learning, working at a couple of zoos and universities around the country.

I started making cakes because I wanted to be able to make my own kids' birthday cakes. I found that I really enjoyed it, so I spent my nights and weekends practicing my sugar skills. Making cakes was my way to de-stress after a long day of teaching. Then, a short dance with cancer made me rethink how I was spending my days. I decided to quit teaching and spend my time creating cakes for people's best days.

Cakeapotamus is about to celebrate its third anniversary. We specialize in odd and unusual cake requests, and we also host birthday parties at the bakery. I'm fortunate that the bakery only does custom orders; I was able to stop offering walk-in retail within our first year of business. This allows me to attend every one of my kids' awards days, field trips, and doctor appointments—something I couldn't do when I was teaching full-time.

If you'd like to check out the whimsy happening at Cakeapotamus, you can see some of my work and pictures of our events on our social media:

Instagram: **www.instagram.com/cakeapotamus**
Facebook: **www.facebook.com/cakeapotamus**
Pinterest: **www.pinterest.com/cakeapotamus**

If you like the photos and you'd like to order from Cakeapotamus, I strongly prefer people contact me online. Email me, send me a private message on Facebook, or submit the cake ordering form on **www.cakeapotamus.com**. My email address is **cakeapotamus@gmail.com**

I have been known to ship cookies, small treats, and truffles for dogs, but I've never shipped a cake. If you'd like to order a cake and have me ship it, drop me a note, and I'll see if we can work it out.

IRENE'S DESSERT TABLE

My name is **Irene Cruz**. I tested the recipes Mandi created for this cookbook and worked directly with her to perfect each one. I also baked and decorated the cakes you see in the photos!

A little about me: I have been married to my handsome husband for thirty-four years. Wow, yes! Thirty-four years! We married young and are still going strong. That is a whole story in itself. Our family is growing with two beautiful adult children, one amazing son-in-law, and two adorable grandchildren.

I grew up in Southern California. Yes, I am a total beach girl, the kind that loves to watch the waves and walk on the sand, searching for beautiful seashells.

My passion for food and art started at a very early age. My grandmother had a great influence on my growing interest in food. I spent most of my summers with her. I remember listening to her childhood memories of the food she would help her mother cook, all the traditional foods of her town. I can still picture her expressions as she would describe every meal along with all the steps to create each dish.

When I was ten, I baked my first cake for my oldest brother. I remember this as if it was yesterday. It was a chocolate cake with chocolate frosting, and I piped a happy face on it using whipped cream from a can. I remember how happy he was and how proud I felt.

When it was time to choose a career, without question I chose a food-related field. My education includes restaurant management, baking, and pastry-making. I continue to cultivate my expertise and attend workshops on food preparation, wine, and art. I have worked in many upscale bakeries in Southern California in production management. I taught baking and cake decorating for five years at a local adult school.

My business is very young; it's still growing and developing. I have recently taken part in several collaborations, and my work has been published in magazines and on blogs. My future plans are to have a space to continue to inspire and teach the art of sugar and baking. There will be workshops to teach about the appreciation of wine and a studio to cater desserts and specialty cakes. I have lots to look forward to and am ready to begin my new journey in this food world I love so much.

The *Gilmore Girls* show is close to my heart. I have fond memories of watching the show with my daughter. She and I always looked forward to curling up on the sofa in anticipation for that week's show. (This was long before Netflix.) I think we related to the show because I was a young mother: strong, independent, silly, and totally addicted to coffee. My daughter: studious, smart, and a teenager at the time. We loved the relationship Rory and Lorelai had. We could totally relate to it. My daughter was going to college along with Rory, and I was working on my career just like Lorelai. The show brought us joy during our busy lives. Once a week, we looked forward to spending girl time together, watching our favorite show, *Gilmore Girls*.

See photos of my cakes on Instragram:
www.instagram.com/irenesdesserttable

BOOSTERS & RECIPE CONTRIBUTORS

Scott Symes

Location: Silver Lake, California

Scott is originally from Oklahoma City but has called Los Angeles home for the last sixteen years. He lives in the Silver Lake neighborhood of LA with his partner Art and their two French Bulldog puppies, Oliver and Charlie. Scott works in Burbank for the top entertainment payroll solutions company in the industry.

As a young kid, Scott was a very picky eater—one of those "food can't touch other food on the plate" and "eat only one food at a time" kind of picky. Canned fruits and veggies over fresh produce, TV dinners over home cooked meals, and so on. Ironically, Scott's mom was and still is a fantastic cook.

Thankfully, over time, Scott learned to appreciate all kinds of food. Today, Scott enjoys cooking and loves getting recipes from his mom that taste great and are easy to make. He also is addicted to the Food Network but embarrassingly admits he has rarely ever actually tried to make something he's seen on any of his favorite shows.

Heather Burson

Location: Suttons Bay, Michigan

Favorite *Gilmore Girls* Episode: "A-Tisket, A-Tasket"

Heather is a baker at heart, learning the secrets of the kitchen from a long line of Italian women, who instilled an instinct for knowing when a dish is "just right." That same instinct pushed her to leave a radio broadcasting career and follow a nagging "What If?" to start a bakery of her own. *In omnia paratus!* Heather is now the chef/owner of Third Coast Bakery and lives in Suttons Bay, Michigan, with her flannel-loving, baseball-cap-wearing, official taste-tester husband, JD, and their two cats. She first started watching *Gilmore Girls* on the CW and still enjoys regular visits to Stars Hollow via Netflix.

Third Coast Bakery is a full-service, dedicated, allergen-safe bakery in Suttons Bay, Michigan. The bakery specializes in creating delicious gluten-free, dairy-free, soy-free, and vegan baked goods, offering a menu that covers everything from bread and crackers to wedding cakes, and yes, even the inspired Blueberry Shortcake.

www.thirdcoastbakedgoods.com

Shehzeen & Mehreen Ahmed

Location: Shehzeen—New York, New York
Mehreen—Farmington Hills, Michigan

Favorite *Gilmore Girls* Episode:
Shehzeen—"Friday Night's Alright For Fighting"
Mehreen—"You Jump, I Jump, Jack"

Shehzeen and Mehreen are a Michigan-born-and-raised sister duo who are avid bakers. Like many of us, their love of cooking started at those family meals. They have been *Gilmore Girls* fanatics for years. Much like Sookie, they like experimenting in the kitchen and using their friends and family to test the new treats they dream up!

In 2012, their father was diagnosed with brain cancer, and they used food as a way to keep him happy and positive throughout his fight. His love of food encouraged them to create fun and innovative recipes in the kitchen. Not only did they come up with some delicious meals, they were also able to spend quality time with their dad during his battle, as he proudly watched them in the kitchen. They are dedicating the five recipes they have contributed to this cookbook in memory of their fun-loving and food-loving father.

Barbie Saylor Kurt

Location: Northern Virginia

Favorite *Gilmore Girls* Episode: "The Bracebridge Dinner"

Barbie Saylor Kurt is a nature girl at heart, and that mindset influences everything she makes, as a home cook and as the founder, maker, and designer behind heritage & belle, a line of nature-inspired jewelry, soy candles, and organic body and bath products.

"I adore things with a little age, naturally occurring elements, the patina of history, and a great backstory—movies, music, books, jewelry, wine, cheese, fashion, design elements, and people."

A ~~vegetarian~~ coffee addict, Barbie maintains a ~~healthy lifestyle~~ huge collection of whimsical mugs ~~by cooking with organic, whole foods, and practicing yoga in her home studio~~ and can often be found at Whole Foods with a cart full of organic dark roast and truffles.

"I'm of the mindset that real is better—and yes, that includes dark chocolate, butter, and sugar, but in moderation. I'm super passionate about knowing how my food was grown and sourced. This desire for cleaner living is what inspired me to start heritage & belle."

Barbie lives with her husband, country singer-songwriter Scott Kurt, in Northern Virginia, where they share their home and love of all things Gilmore with their five rescue cats.

Connect with her on Twitter & Instagram: **@BarbieKurt14**

Gerome Huerta

Location: Los Angeles, California

Gerome is a California native, born in the San Francisco East Bay Area. He was raised by Southerners and a first generation Mexican immigrant, which made for interesting food habits at an early age, among other things. He's now been a resident of the Los Angeles area for twenty years.

Jack of many trades, master of none (well, maybe sarcasm), Gerome was a retail sales and operations guru for many years but eventually discovered his passion in and for food. After breaking out of the corporate mold, he now enjoys being an amateur cook who loves to create and recreate recipes with his own spin. Gerome headed his own restaurant for a while; he's hoping to return to it after working and learning more in the industry.

Aside from food, Gerome finds passion in other interests such as LGBTQ community rights, animal/dog rights and rescue, and collecting classic cars. He's also interested in nearly anything internet-related, staying up nights as late as humanly possible (but able to function the next day) and people gathering . . . with (more) food.

Tony Escarcega

Location: Los Angeles, California

Favorite *Gilmore Girls* Episode: "Raincoats and Recipes"

Tony was born and raised in southern Arizona. It was there that he learned to cook from his mom and grandmothers. Tony instantly loved cooking and being in the kitchen. After learning the basics, he continued learning on his own—exploring new techniques and methods, becoming more creative and adventurous with food and recipes. Tony honed his skills while being a short order cook in Target's Food Avenue and a brief stint in federal prison as a cook.

Tony's first love has always been film, and he has a BA in media arts. His other passion is food. Tony would like to open a restaurant/gourmet food shop. Tony enjoys photography as well and is branching out now to include food photography.

When asked if he wanted to contribute to this cookbook, Tony was ecstatic to be able to create a recipe. It gave him the opportunity to create something based on a show he is a fan of, in a medium he is passionate about.

Tony makes his home in the Los Angeles area, steps from the Stars Hollow sets.

RECIPE TESTER BIOS

Art Gonzales Jr.

Location: Silver Lake, California

Art is a native Californian who grew up in the San Fernando Valley. At an early age, he discovered he had a love for animals that has remained to this day. Art was fortunate enough to find a way to make a career out of working with animals and, for the last twenty years, has been an animal keeper at the Los Angeles Zoo. Through his service there, he has cared for almost every animal found on the zoo grounds and takes every opportunity he can to talk with patrons about the importance of animal education and conservation. Currently he cares for the "hoof stock" animals, and one of his favorites is two-year-old Bomani, the first okapi born at the LA Zoo.

When not at the zoo, Art likes spending time with his partner Scott, and their two French Bulldogs, Oliver and Charlie. Art has two adult sons and can't wait to meet his first grandson who will be born this fall. Admittedly, he doesn't really cook but loves to eat and, after hearing about some of the recipes his friend Kristi has been talking about, can't wait to have Scott try them out at home.

Shelby Sloan

Location: Rapid City, South Dakota

Favorite *Gilmore Girls* Episode: "Those Are Strings, Pinocchio"

Vicious trollop with wilderness skills.

Alfred Rubalcaba

Location: Corona, California

Alfred Rubalcaba was born in sunny Southern California and raised in the San Gabriel Valley and North Orange County area of the state. He is an admissions counselor for a private university. Helping and guiding young people as they enter college is something he enjoys and excels at. He is also a student, currently working on his master's degree in organizational leadership.

Alfred and his three younger brothers were raised by a single mother who had neither talent nor desire for cooking. As a result, the kitchen stove and oven were perpetually clean and spot-free. Alfred's mom fed the family with many salads, fresh fruit, vegetables, and occasionally simple items such as grilled chicken and fish. As the years went on, Alfred realized there was a world of delectable items out there just waiting to be tasted and enjoyed. Now as an adult, Alfred has had the opportunity to enjoy some of the best restaurants and finer cuisine. He also enjoys a great "hole in the wall."

Along with trying new restaurants, Alfred enjoys spending time with his small group of friends and his family—especially his three nephews, three nieces, and godson.

Bridget & Shawn Kushiyama

Location: Houston, Texas

Favorite *Gilmore Girls* Episode: Bridget – "The Deer Hunters"
Shawn – "You Jump, I Jump, Jack"

Shawn and Bridget started dating in 2009 and got married in September 2014. He grew up in New Jersey, and she grew up in Louisiana. They met in Louisiana while finishing up school and then wound up in Houston because of Shawn's job. One of their favorite things to do together is to cook. Every anniversary, they attempt to cook a dish they've never cooked before. They've made lobster rolls, ramen, duck with gnocchi, and soup dumplings. They found out, right before Christmas 2015, that they were expecting a baby boy due in August 2016! They had some trouble thinking of a name, and the only name they ever liked was "Logan," which seemed appropriate.

Sarah Lea Phelps

Location: New Jersey

Favorite *Gilmore Girls* Episode: "You Jump, I Jump, Jack"

Amateur baker, macaroni and cheese aficionado, Sarah Lea recently moved to the suburbs where she happily discovered kitchens there were larger than her entire city apartment. Other hobbies include reading, traveling, and hiding in closets to scare her husband for her own sick pleasure.

Find her on Instagram: **@sarahlea13**

Revs. Krystal & John Leedy

Location: Austin, Texas

Favorite *Gilmore Girls* Episode: Krystal – "We've Got Magic to Do"
John – "You Jump, I Jump, Jack"

Krystal and John Leedy are both Presbyterian Church (USA) pastors. They began watching *Gilmore Girls* early on in their relationship. Because of their love for ritual, each year when the first cold snap arrives in their hometown of Austin, they begin watching all the episodes of *Gilmore Girls* in order, quoting along and laughing with the quick-witted humor and heart-wrenching drama that is this amazing show.

When they are not watching *Gilmore Girls*, John enjoys camping and playing the bagpipes, and Krystal loves cross-stitching and playing the djembe. Because they appreciate the intelligence, strength, and humor of the *Gilmore Girls* characters, they decided to name their first-born daughter Lorelai. Their dog, a Jack Russell Terrier named Cricket, is a big fan of Paul Anka and runs up to the TV every time he makes an appearance. As ministers, John and Krystal also appreciate the down-to-earth and winsomely irreverent Reverend Skinner and Rabbi Barans who are part of the daily life in Stars Hollow. From time to time, Krystal will send John on a late-night run to pick up some Twinkies, and now, thanks to this great cookbook, they can make them at home.

Katlyn Allenson & Teri Patzwald

Location: Katlyn—Tampa, Florida
Teri—Ocala, Florida

Favorite *Gilmore Girls* Episode: Katlyn—"You Jump, I Jump, Jack"
Teri—"Love and War and Snow"

As a mother-daughter combo, Katlyn and Teri have been baking together for as long as they can remember. Katlyn's mom, Teri, gave her all of the basics and support, so now she puts her own little twist on classic sweets.

Even though Katlyn moved away, the two still get together for every holiday to make family favorites or test out new recipes. From candy-filled cakes for Katlyn's nephew's birthday, to a dessert bar at her wedding, to holiday platters, baking together is something they always look forward to doing.

Watching *Gilmore Girls* became a staple in their family, just like baking. It is one of those activities that always brings out a smile, one they hope to share with future generations.

Amanda True

Location: Maple Valley, Washington

Favorites *Gilmore Girls* Episode: "The Bracebridge Dinner"

Amanda is a wife and stay-at-home mommy to two fantastic and crazy little boys, ages three and six months! In her spare time—on the rare occasion when she gets some—she loves reading, baking, and of course, watching *Gilmore Girls*.

Her favorite episode of the show *would* be "Raincoats and Recipes," where Luke and Lorelai kiss for the first time, but it is ruined for her by the Rory and Dean storyline. Because of that, her favorite is "The Bracebridge Dinner." According to Amanda, "There is something fun and magical about that episode, in spite of Rune."

Ryan Elizabeth Russell

Location: San Jose, California

Favorite *Gilmore Girls* Episode: "The Incredible Sinking Lorelais"

Ryan is a 911 dispatcher who also works part time at La Rochelle Winery in Kenwood, California. She loves and is extremely passionate about both jobs. When not working, Ryan likes to travel, drink, and eat.

Melissa McAndrews

Location: San Jose, California

Favorite *Gilmore Girls* Episode: "Last Week Fights, This Week Tights"

Melissa is a 911 dispatcher with her local fire department. She spends her spare time doing photography, going to baseball games, sewing, or just hanging out with friends, eating good food, and drinking good drinks. She loves the beach and tries to travel at least once a year to somewhere she's never been. She happened upon *Gilmore Girls* while flipping through TV channels one day and loved it immediately. It was difficult for her to choose a favorite episode; she loves too many of them! It came down to two. She loves Lorelai's birthday episode with the (almost) largest pizza in the world because of the Jimmy Choo conversation Lorelai has with Richard and the whole pizza coordination fiasco. But Liz and TJ's wedding won out—because it's when Luke finally accepts that he has feelings for Lorelai. She is very excited to be part of this cookbook and can't wait to try all the recipes!

Kendall Gibson

Location: Baton Rouge, Louisiana

Favorite *Gilmore Girls* Episode: "They Shoot Gilmores, Don't They?"

University Spanish instructor by day; actor-writer-baker by night. Prone to accents and wanderlust. Lover of anything written by Lin-Manuel Miranda or Aaron Sorkin. Classic rock fan. Graduate of Florida State. Vonnegut said everything better than she ever could. "So it goes . . . "

To learn more about Kendall, visit her website: **www.wanderingflamingo.wix.com/home**

Brianne Wetzel

Location: Frisco, Texas

Favorite *Gilmore Girls* Episode: "You Jump, I Jump, Jack"

Brianne is a married mother of two with baby #3 on the way. She's a nutritionist, life/wellness coach, and a business development coach. Her passion is helping people create freedom for their families.

To learn more about Brianne, visit her website: **www.briannewetzel.com**

Nicky Krieger-Loos

Location: Dudelange, Luxembourg

Favorite *Gilmore Girls* Episode: "Last Week Fights, This Week Tights"

Nicky's family has loved the *Gilmore Girls* right from the beginning, and they all keep re-watching the whole series again and again! She can relate to many characters of the show in different ways: like Lorelai and Rory, she loves coffee! Combine Lorelai's creativity and Luke's ability to fix anything: that's Nicky. Just like Emily, she loves to organize big, fancy parties and plan every detail from food to table settings and decorations—her biggest one being a buffet dinner for 150 guests. Nicky is also somewhat similar to Kirk in that she can take on many different jobs. And finally, people say she's a pretty decent cook, just like Sookie.

This project combined three of her favorite things: *Gilmore Girls*, family, and cooking. That's why she jumped at the chance to be part of it. She tested out the Pot Roast recipe with her two beautiful daughters and enjoyed it with her whole family.

Each of them can truly eat like a Gilmore.

Karla Kelly Nickerson

Location: San Diego, California

Karla was born a Midwestern girl just outside Chicago, Illinois. Shortly thereafter, her family moved to Iowa, land of corn and small-town values. She remembers visiting her "Nanny" and the smells of homemade crescent rolls and rhubarb pie coming from her kitchen. When she was eight years old, she moved to Canada. A small town named "Streetsville" allowed her to grow up in simple times where she was able to go home from school every day for lunch and enjoy Campbell's® chicken noodle soup and raspberries off the vine! Her mom (who never worked outside the home) preparing those lunches will always be one of her favorite childhood memories. At eighteen, she moved to San Diego, California where she met and married her hubby of thirty-three years. She considers herself a home-style cook of simple meals to be enjoyed around the dinner table with family. She has learned to cook healthier meals thanks to living in Southern California, where healthy eating is always at the forefront. Karla loves being a mom and nana, living in San Diego, the ocean/beach, wearing flip-flops year-round, and reading crime novels on the backyard patio. She believes in angels, unconditional love, longtime friendships, and that "simple" is better!

Shannon Huffman

Location: North Pole, Alaska

Favorite *Gilmore Girls* episode: "Last Week Fights, This Week Tights"

Shannon is a married mom of two teenagers. Originally from Flint, Michigan, she now lives in North Pole, Alaska. She works for a nonprofit and is also a current student with Vizio Online Makeup Academy.

She chose the episode she did because it starts to show the beginning of the Luke and Lorelai romance and because TJ's comic relief is priceless.

YouTube channel: **www.youtube.com/channel/UClDtpqsLLf9_sKKVf_g84Hw**

Blog: **www.simplyshannonblog.com**

Emily Moeller

Location: Charleston, South Carolina

Favorite *Gilmore Girls* Episode: "The Road Trip to Harvard"

Emily loves anything that revolves around the outdoors, college football, and breakfast food. She's currently a graduate student and a Leslie Knope wannabe.

REFERENCE GUIDE

Abbreviations

t = teaspoon

T = tablespoon

oz = ounce

g = gram

c = cup

pt = pint

qt = quart

lb = pound

Ingredients

Butter = salted butter

Sugar = white, granulated sugar

Flour = all-purpose flour

Milk = whole milk

Vanilla = pure vanilla extract

Charlie P. Bear
KITCHEN FLOOR PATROL OFFICER

Basic Equipment

Ninety percent of the recipes in this book can be made using this list of equipment.

If you're just beginning to equip your kitchen, investing in the items on this list will enable you to cook nearly everything, not just in this book, but in most any cookbook.

If you're on a budget, many of these items can be found very inexpensively at thrift stores and garage sales.

Dutch oven

Saucepan

Frying pan

Oven

Electric mixer

Blender and/or food processor

Coffeemaker

9x14-inch baking pan

8x8-inch baking pan

Cookie sheet

Standard 8-inch pie plate

Jumbo muffin pan

Candy thermometer

Meat thermometer (instant-read variety for checking temperatures toward end of cooking time)

Heat-resistant rubber spatula

Slotted spoon

Wire whisk

Sharp chef's knife

Sharp serrated knife

Vegetable peeler

Grater

Strainer

Tongs

Pitcher

Mixing bowls (various sizes)

Measuring cups (for dry ingredients)

2-cup measuring cup (for liquids)

Measuring spoons

Cooling rack(s)

Piping bag

Drink shaker

Jigger

Citrus squeezer or juicer

Specialized Equipment

A few recipes included in this book require specialized equipment.

Pizzelles: Pizzelle maker

Chocolate Chocolate Chocolate Ice Cream: Ice cream maker

Mini Lemon Bundt Cakes: Mini Bundt pan

Homemade Twinkies: Twinkie pan

Deep Fried Turkey:

32-quart heavy-gauge stainless steel turkey fryer stockpot (a larger size may work)

14-inch propane-powered high pressure outdoor burner

Propane tank

ABC-rated fire extinguisher

Heavy-duty rubber safety gloves

Safety face mask

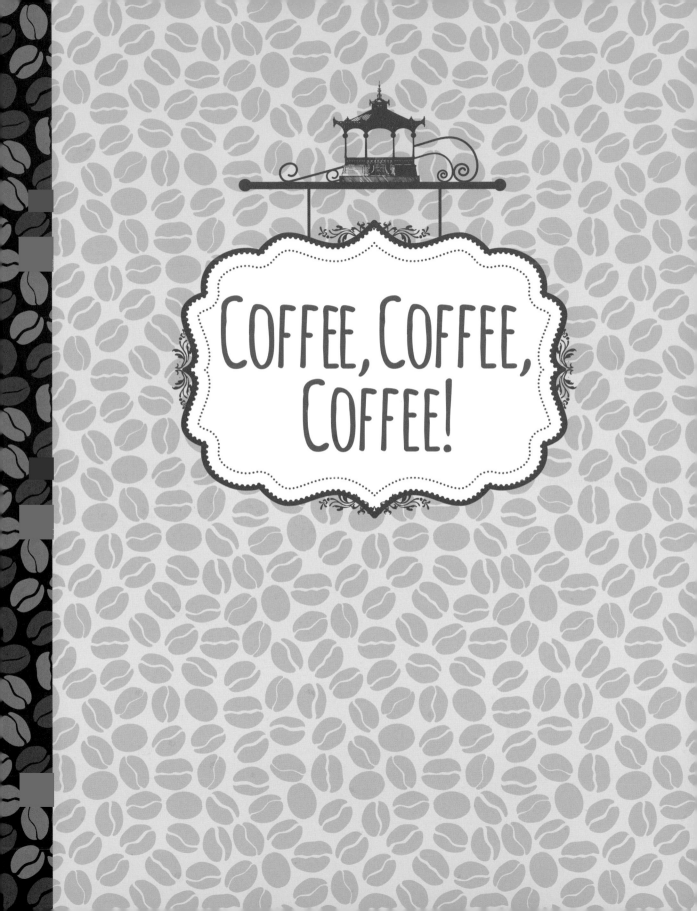

EMBER QUILLWEB

My coffee intake not only matches Lorelai Gilmore's, but at times raises her two cups and a biscotti.

I really like coffee, but what makes me such an authority on it? Well, aside from years of being in a serious relationship with it, I also did my time at a café where I learned a lot, not only about different processes and kinds of coffee, but also about people's tastes and preferences. I discovered that some people drink coffee solely for the caffeine and do not like the taste, thus, some folks need to sugar it up just to get it down.

Sugar—oh boy, I'll try to contain my rant on the stuff—but sugar completely masks the taste of coffee. I really urge people to reintroduce themselves to coffee without all the flavored syrups, creamers, and sugar—they are nice for a treat, but learn to get a taste for what a good cup of coffee should be before you start to alter it. You might just find you're really a hot blonde who doesn't like sand.

So, Let's Talk About the Basics Everyone Who Makes Coffee at Home Needs to Know . . .

COFFEE 101

7 Steps To A Great Cup Of Coffee At Home: For the purpose of making this simple to follow, I will be referring to the at-home drip coffeemaker. But every point I touch on is applicable and recommended for whatever your brewing method of choice is.

Name Your Machine

Not only is it a Gilmore thing to name your appliances, it will give your inanimate object a sense of belonging, and it might even perform better for it. Actually, since a coffeemaker brews and flows water through itself, it's not that inanimate. With that said, I will sometimes refer to the coffee machine as "Bailey."

Give Bailey a Bath

Seriously, when was the last time you cleaned your machine? I don't mean the pot, but the actual machine? I won't gross you out with talk on bacteria growth, but you need to give Bailey a bath once a month. A dirty Bailey affects the taste of your coffee—not only are germs in it but also mineral buildup. Even though you may not see it, it's there and leeches into each brew, altering the taste, as well as making your machine brew more slowly.

Cleaning the machine sounds like a lot of work but it isn't. Put on an episode of *Gilmore Girls*. Now run a brew cycle for an almost full pot with a vinegar and water mix (50/50 ratio is good; more parts vinegar if you're super grossed out). Don't wander off, for half way through the "brew" cycle, pause or turn off the machine to let the heated remaining solution sit and do its work. Three-fourths through the *Gilmore* episode (about 30 minutes), brew the rest of the solution. When finished, pour out the solution, and brew a full pot of just water. Pour that out, and run one more just-water cycle, so Bails is good and rinsed. Woo-hoo! Bailey is feeling good now! Though you need to do this once a month, each day you should be cleaning your pot and the removable parts. Leave the machine's lid open when not in use to help keep the machine dry and mold away.

Use Filtered Water

You are not letting the good coffee times flow if you are using tap or well water, which both have contaminants and added oddities in them, as well as bacteria; all of which can mess with the longevity of your machine and your innards. Think about it: coffee is mainly water. Do your Bailey, body, and palate a favor—use filtered water! Oh, and that little carbon filter thing some machines have does not cut it. Use either water from a robust home filtration system, or store-bought filtered water.

The Grind

No, I am not talking about a 90s dance show. I am talking about your beans. Did you get the right grind for your machine? This can affect the taste due to the way water extracts the flavor during the brew. Find out what type of grindage your machine calls for. For drip machines using flat-bottomed filters, go with a medium grind; more fine for cone filters. Metal/mesh filters need a courser grind.

Measurement

Not all of us are such pros like Luke where we can eyeball the amount needed to brew. If you are like me, first thing in the A.M., I need all the direction I can get. The recommended dosage is 2 tablespoons coffee for every 6 ounces of water. You can start there and experiment with more or less coffee and see how it goes.

Find Your Soul Coffee Mate

You need to discover what your taste is when it comes to coffee. Do you like it acidic, dark, cowboy-drinking-it-from-a-tin-cup strong, or do you prefer chocolate/caramel notes, maybe a smooth body (va va to the voom)! Have fun and experiment with different kinds; it took me years until I found my go-to brand. It will help if you understand the roast terms when picking out coffee, and keep in mind that each company has its own roast levels. Typically, light roasts, which literally have been lightly roasted, tend to be more acidic, even grainy. Common names for light roasts are New England and Cinnamon (not the cat, R.I.P.). Next are medium roasts, which tend to be more balanced and smoother. Other names for medium roasts are Breakfast, Regular, and American. Lastly, we have the dark roast. Since dark roast means it has been roasted longer than the aforementioned, the flavor can be bitter and smoky. Common names you'll find for this roast are French, Italian, Spanish, and Continental.

Storage

The key to keeping your caffeine love affair from going stale is to protect it from air and moisture. If you keep your coffee in the fridge, take it out. It is not 1955. Get it out of there, and keep it in a sealed jar. The fridge actually creates moisture in the coffee. I personally don't like to even keep coffee in plastic or metal containers and certainly not in the bag it came in due to air exposure. I use a big glass mason jar, and it stays nice and fresh and looks quite stylish on my counter.

If you follow these basic steps on coffee-making, you will be well on your way to brewing a cup not even Kirk would unwillingly put seven sweetener packets into. Now then, on to some coffee drink recipes you can make at home!

A CUP O' LUKE'S

In order to make a great cup of coffee at home that is as close as you can get to a cup at Luke's, you must follow the basics I mentioned above for Coffee 101. The only other item you need in order to hit a home-run cup like Luke's is to find the right type of coffee to suit your taste (but know that diners tend to serve medium roasts).

It's that simple. You don't necessarily have to go searching and paying top dollar for some artisan coffee to get a decent diner-worthy cup. Let's face it, diner coffee is its own breed of coffee, just like gas station coffee, just like big-chain coffee places. That's not to say diner coffee is bad; it's just in its own category of coffee.

Luke's coffee should be a light/medium (more on the medium side) roast that's not very acidic. As I mentioned before, medium roasts tend to be more balanced, with a nice body, and are considered the standard Americana of roasts. Oooh . . . kinda like Luke! So follow the basics, go with a Breakfast Blend–type of roast, and don't be surprised if, after tasting the difference in your coffee, you soon find yourself wearing a backward baseball cap.

*Please note: For the following recipes, I have listed two ways to makes them — *The Sookie Way* and *The Lorelai Way*.

For *The Sookie Way*, it is assumed you have an espresso machine, a sense of belonging in a kitchen, and you possibly own a cute chef's jacket.

For *The Lorelai Way*, in your kitchen you have a functional sink, you may have experience warming up socks in the oven, and if you haven't already, you will be welcoming two new best friends into your home: instant espresso and a milk frother. You will need a milk frother to aerate the milk to get foam for some of the recipes below. Frothers can be used for other kitchen tasks like making milk shakes and sauces—plus they are inexpensive to boot! <waving my frothing wand like a coffee maestro> Let the coffee recipes commence!

THE COLLEGE LATTE

Well, it seems once Rory got to Yale, her coffee drink got a little upgraded. She would still get coffee, but she is also ordering macchiatos, cappuccinos—well, when she could afford them. A great college campus to-go coffee drink is a latte since, due to all the milk, it can double as a meal.

You can easily make a basic latte at home: it's just espresso and steamed milk, topped with foam. So, if you're in a rush, skint, or both, have a latte—the meal substitute of the college world.

The Sookie Way:

Espresso

Milk

Well, it's easy-peasy The Sookie Way, for you will have in your possession a fancy at-home espresso machine.

Basically just steam up your milk of choice (ideally around 140°F), pull some shots into a cup (one shot for small, two for medium/large), hold back the foam as you pour the steamed milk into the cup, dollop with some foam, and then head to your nearest library and smell a book or two, or three, or four.

The Lorelai Way:

Instant espresso

Milk

Measure espresso and milk: Pre-measure espresso (follow the package's recommended measurement) and set aside. Using your mug as a measuring glass, fill it with milk of choice. (Please note: for the following heating method, the heavier the milk the better, thicker foam you will get.)

Heat milk: Pour milk into saucepan and heat on stove. Armed with your magic milk-frothing wand, aerate the milk as it heats with one hand, and use your other to add your instant espresso to your mug.

Assemble and serve: Take care not to burn the milk; when it seems hot and frothy, hold back foam, as you pour a little into your mug (you can use a large spoon for this). Stir to dissolve the instant espresso powder. Again, holding back foam, fill rest of mug with steamed milk and then dollop with some foam. Voilà! A latte.

MOCHA CHOCOLATE CARAMEL WHIRL-A-CHINO

This is a great beverage to have on days of reconciliation. It's basically a cappuccino that had an intense fling with chocolate, while seeing some caramel at the same time—then tried to cover the whole ordeal up with extra whipped cream.

The Sookie Way:

Caramel Sauce:

1 c	Brown sugar, packed
½ c	Butter
¼ c	Milk
1 t	Vanilla

Mocha Sauce:

2–3 oz	Chocolate, high quality, 60–85% cacao

Whipped Cream:

½ c	Heavy cream
1 T	Superfine sugar
¼ t	Vanilla

Latte:

1 c	Milk
1 oz	Espresso shot(s)
	Chocolate chips and/or chocolate shavings, for garnish

The Lorelai Way:

2–3 oz	Mocha Sauce (see above) or chocolate syrup
1–2 oz	Caramel Sauce (see above)
1	serving instant espresso
8 oz	Whole milk
1 can	Whipped cream
	Chocolate chips and/or chocolate shavings, for garnish

Make the Caramel Sauce: Combine brown sugar, butter, and milk in a saucepan and bring to a boil until thickened. Remove from heat and stir in the vanilla.

Make the Mocha Sauce: Melt the chocolate (make sure there's enough for drizzle too) in a saucepan over medium heat.

Make the Whipped Cream: Add heavy cream, superfine sugar, and vanilla to a small mixing bowl. With a mixer set on medium speed, beat until stiff peaks form. Set aside.

Make the Latte: Pour some Mocha Sauce into an 8-ounce mug (about 1–2 tablespoons for a medium-size mug). Pour some caramel sauce in there as well, 1 tablespoon, more or less depending on how sweet your teeth are. Steam up milk of choice, making sure to froth well. Pull two shots into mug, then "free" pour milk into mug (this means don't hold back the foam; pour it as is—thus the body of the drink is light and frothy)—be sure to leave about 2 inches of room. Top with extra Whipped Cream and drizzle Mocha and Caramel Sauces over the whipped tower. Now, sprinkle some chocolate shavings and/or chips over it. If you have plans that evening, cancel them. Nothing is going to be more exciting than this.

Prep the mug: Take an 8-ounce mug and fill with milk to measure. Pour milk into saucepan. Before you start heating the milk, be sure to put about 1–2 tablespoons Mocha Sauce/chocolate syrup into mug, as well as the same amount of Caramel Sauce (for syrups use 2–3 pumps), then add the instant espresso (follow the package's recommended measurement).

Heat milk: In a small saucepan, over medium-high heat, heat milk, using frothing wand to make it nice and, well, frothy. Don't overcook your milk.

Mix in milk: Pour a little of the heated milk into mug to mix up the sauce/syrups and espresso powder. Free pour (don't hold back the foam) the frothed milk into the mug, leaving about 2 inches of room.

Serve: Top with extra whipped cream, Mocha Sauce/chocolate syrup, Caramel Sauce (if you have it), chocolate chips, and hey, since you're home, anything else in the chocolate family you have laying around that you feel would crown this achievement—throw it on there! Now enjoy your time together, for once the morning comes and you see it un-whirled and un-whipped, you'll be moving on.

CANDY CANE COFFEE

No need to fret and rant when your local fancy coffee-drink-makin' go-to pulls the seasonal goods off the menu and you can't bribe your way into getting even a "misplaced" canister sent your way. Now you can make this seasonal delight in your home, any time of year!

The Sookie Way:

8 oz	Coffee

Peppermint Syrup:

1 c	Water
1 c	Sugar
½–1 T	Mint extract

Whipped Cream:

½ c	Heavy cream
1 T	Superfine sugar
¼ t	Vanilla

Peppermint candies and/or candy canes, for garnish

Mint leaves, for garnish

Make Peppermint Syrup*: Bring water and sugar to a boil, then reduce heat, and stir until the sugar has dissolved. Stir in mint extract. Remove from heat and let cool. Mixture can be stored in the fridge up to 2 weeks.

Make Whipped Cream: Add heavy cream, superfine sugar, and vanilla to a small mixing bowl. With a mixer set on medium speed, beat until stiff peaks form. Set aside.

Crush peppermints: Take peppermint candies and put into a baggy. Borrow TJ's Mystic Hammer and, on a safe surface, let out those feelings you have about strawberries no longer being in season on the bag of candies until they are crushed into little sprinkle pieces.

Assemble and serve: Put about ½ teaspoon Peppermint Syrup in mug and fill with coffee, leaving 1–2 inches of room. Sip to see if more Peppermint Syrup is desired. Then top with Whipped Cream, crushed peppermints, and/or garnish with a candy cane and mint leaf. Now find a comfy arm chair, wrap yourself in a cozy blanket, and enjoy!

The Lorelai Way:

Store-bought whipped cream

Store-bought peppermint syrup

Same as above, except substitute the homemade whipped cream and Peppermint Syrup <whispers, "peppermint"> for store-bought. (Though the syrup is so easy to make, go for it!) While enjoying this holly-jolly coffee, you may have an urge to decorate your living room with many, many artificial evergreen trees, so you might want to clear some space prior.

*Note: *If you wanted to make the Peppermint Syrup out of actual candy canes, well, you could, but to avoid acquiring merely the whisper of peppermint, you'll need more than just the three Lorelai dunks into her coffee. In fact, you will need about 10–12 candy canes, standard size. Put them into a pot with 1 cup of water, bring to a boil, then remove from heat and let cool. Now you have some actual candy cane syrup—add in small amounts to your coffee to find preferred taste. Be prepared for your sinuses to be quite clear upon drinking.*

Cocktails, Mocktails
& Other Assorted Beverages

THE BIRTHDAY GIRL

To honor the youngest Gilmore at her properly opulent twenty-first birthday party, Emily instructed the bartender to create a custom cocktail, specifically for Rory.

Just like the drink at Rory's party, this cocktail looks very pretty. The pinkish-red tones catch the light and shine as beautifully as Rory's face did when Luke gave her his mother's pearls. But beware—this is a sugary-sweet pink-fest, which tastes more like liquid cotton candy than a birthday cocktail. Drinking too many of these is likely to induce a Kirk-level sugar hangover. Indulge at your own risk!

¼ c	Water, for rim
¼ c	Granulated sugar (for rim)
	Ice
3 oz	Vodka
1 oz	Grenadine
1 oz	Pineapple juice
1 oz	Champagne
1	Maraschino cherry, for garnish

Prep glass: In two small plates or shallow bowls, place water in one, sugar in the other. Using a martini glass, dip the rim of the glass ⅛ inch into the water, then immediately into the sugar. With glass still in sugar, give it a twist while turning the glass upright. Sugar should stick to the rim of the glass in a thin, uniform line.

Mix the drink: Add ice to a shaker until it is half full. Pour in vodka, grenadine, and pineapple juice. Place lid on shaker, and shake until liquids are well blended. Remove shaker lid, add champagne, and gently stir.

Serve: Stain into prepared glass. Garnish with a maraschino cherry. Serve.

Tester—Ryan Elizabeth Russell

FOUNDERS DAY PUNCH

TOWN FAVORITE

On the show, creation of Founders Day Punch is credited to Miss Patty. Over time, we learn that its deceptively delicious, fruity flavor makes it easy to drink while the booze quietly sneaks up on you. Like all the best punch recipes, it's easy to make and disappears quickly.

This punch is a Stars Hollow legend and is served at the quirkiest of town functions. The first it's heard of is during the Firelight Festival when we learn Rachael is a big fan of it, and Liz reminisces with Luke about drinking it in high school.

A few seasons later, the magic of the punch gets passed on to the next generation, rather appropriately, after Old Man Twickham dies. Taylor turns the Twickham House into a museum and diorama, wowing the crowds with pioneering mannequins, while Miss Patty serves up her punch.

It's an instant hit with the newly old-enough-to-drink trio of Paris, Lane, and Rory—however, Rory spends that night on the bathroom floor and wakes up with tile marks on her face.

So . . . while drinking this punch may lead you into a taco-worthy hangover, or a committed relationship with a sexy, blond billionaire, or both—be sure to clean your bathroom before you make it.

3 c	**Passion fruit juice**
1½ c	**Cranberry juice**
1 c	**Pineapple juice**
1 c	**Vodka**
½ c	**Brandy**
1 c	**Sparkling apple cider**
	Ice

Mix punch: Combine passion fruit, cranberry, and pineapple juices in a pitcher or punch bowl. Add vodka and brandy. Stir well, until fully blended. Add sparkling apple cider. Stir gently to combine.

Serve over ice.

Makes 16 (4-ounce) servings.

***Tester**—Ryan Elizabeth Russell*

MARTINI

EMILY'S HOUSE

Though Richard and Emily Gilmore clearly believe the proper procedure for running a household is to leave menial tasks like cooking and cleaning to one's staff, they do, however, show both enthusiasm and skill for mixing cocktails. With drink carts in the living room, on the patio, and in the pool house, they embrace the traditional etiquette and hospitality of offering alcohol to everyone who visits. Even when Emily is charged with teaching high society manners and graces to ten-year-old Charlotte, one of the first bits of wisdom she imparts is how to mix a Martini. Rightly so—a few of these will make any Friday Night Dinner more tolerable.

	Ice
4 oz	Vodka
1½ oz	Vermouth
	Olive, for garnish
	Olive "juice" from the olive jar, optional

Mix the drink: Fill shaker half full of ice. Add vodka and vermouth. Shake vigorously for 1 minute to fully combine and chill the liquids. Stain into a martini glass. Garnish with one large olive or multiple small olives.

Dirty Martini: To make the martini "dirty," add liquid from the olive jar in ½-ounce increments until the taste of it suits you.

SIDECAR

The Sidecar is the drink Emily subtly used to hack away at Lorelai's confidence and comfort the night Logan came to Friday Night Dinner. She well knew Lorelia's drink of choice was a Martini—yet she kept hammering away, asking if Lorelai wanted a Sidecar. Anyone who knows Lorelai knows this just is not her type of drink—but perhaps it's yours. Give it a try. Just be sure to keep an eye on your antique knickknacks while you drink it.

¼ c	Sugar
2	Slices lemon
	Ice
1½ oz	Cognac
¾ oz	Orange liqueur
¾ oz	Lemon juice, freshly squeezed

Prepare the glass: Pour sugar on a plate. Select a martini glass or old-fashioned coupe glass. Rub one slice of lemon around the rim of the glass, then turn glass upside down into sugar. Give the glass a slight twist while turning it upright. The result should be a fine line of sugar around the rim of the glass.

Mix the drink: Fill a shaker half full of ice. Add cognac, orange liqueur, and lemon juice. Shake vigorously for 1 minute. Stain into prepared glass. Garnish with lemon slice. Serve.

GIMLET

This show mentions many old-fashioned cocktails throughout the series—perhaps to add to the "old money" feel of the Gilmore name, or perhaps to breathe some newness into these old favorites. This particular cocktail is like Emily Gilmore herself; at first impression, it's elegant, feminine, slightly sweet, but after some time in its company, it starts playing mind games, making you question your life choices. Drink up!

2 T	Water
2 T	Granulated sugar
	Ice
3 oz	Gin
1½ oz	Lime juice, freshly squeezed
1	Lime wedge, for garnish

Make Simple Syrup: Combine water and sugar in small saucepan. Over medium heat, stir until sugar is fully dissolved and a syrup-like liquid forms. Remove from heat and let cool for 5 minutes. This is your simple syrup.

Mix cocktail: Half-fill a shaker with ice. Add the simple syrup, gin, and lime juice. Shake vigorously for 1–2 minutes. Stain into glass. Attach lime wedge to edge of glass. Serve.

BLOODY MARY

The Harvard vs. Yale game was one of the few times Emily and Richard seemed relatable—for both Lorelai and the show's viewers. They were happy and excited, dressed up in blue (complete with sassy anti-Harvard buttons), out in the fresh air, eager to watch their team play. Although, their extravagant pregame setup and spread may have ruined our own tailgating experiences forever. Who can compete with a fully stocked trailer, awning, picnic table, great food, and a servant or two? Not me. But we've got the very best part of the whole day right here: Emily's Bloody Marys!

	Kosher salt
	Lemon wedge
	Ice
½ oz	Lemon juice, freshly squeezed
½ oz	Lime juice, freshly squeezed
5 oz	Tomato juice
2 oz	Vodka
¼ t	Hot sauce, recommend Tabasco®
¼ t	Worcestershire sauce
1 t	Horseradish, "prepared" style
dash	Celery salt
dash	Paprika
dash	Black pepper
1	Celery stalk, with leaves attached
1	Toothpick
1	Large green olive

Prepare the glass: Pour kosher salt onto a plate. Select a pint glass or beer glass. To moisten the rim, rub the lemon wedge around the entire rim of the glass. Turn glass upside down onto salt. Twist glass while bringing it upright. This should produce a thin, even line of salt around the rim. Fill glass ⅔-full with ice.

Mix: In a shaker or small pitcher, combine lemon juice, lime juice, tomato juice, vodka, hot sauce, Worcestershire sauce, and horseradish. Stir until all ingredients are fully blended. Add celery salt, paprika, and black pepper. Stir again to combine.

Assemble: Pour cocktail into prepared glass. Insert celery stalk (leaves should come up 2–3 inches above rim of glass; cut stalk as needed). Insert toothpick into the side of the olive and rest it on top of the cocktail. Serve.

AUTUMN SANGRIA

Lorelai Leigh Gilmore, who we know as "Rory," turned 16 on October 8, 2000. Her first party, elaborately thrown by her grandmother, resulted in disappointment and hurt feelings. Thankfully, her party the next night rekindled all of her birthday cheer. The simple, at-home shindig, thrown by her mother and Sookie, included all of the colorful townspeople, her best friend Lane, and ultimately, her grandparents.

This was the alcoholic beverage being served that night—because a pitcher of sangria can bring smiles to many faces, for only a few dollars. It's the perfect crowd-pleaser for anyone on a budget!

1	**750-ml bottle wine, red blend**
¼ c	**Pomegranate seeds**
½ c	**Halved red grapes**
1	**Pear, cored, cubed**
2	**Mandarin oranges, sliced and halved**
1	**Apple, cored, cubed**
¼ c	**Pomegranate juice**
½ c	**Brandy**
1 c	**Sparkling apple cider**
4	**Cinnamon sticks**
	Ice

Mix Sangria: Combine wine, fruits, and pomegranate juice in a medium pitcher. Stir in brandy. Refrigerate for 4–6 hours.

Serve: Gently stir in sparkling apple cider. Garnish with cinnamon sticks. Serve over ice.

Makes 6–8 servings.

Tester*—Alfred Rubalcaba*

Eat Like a Gilmore

WHITE RUSSIAN

TOWN FAVORITE

What do you do when the oven is broken and your casserole is sitting in it, barely breaking a sweat? You pop open whatever pre-packaged treat you have in the fridge and pour yourself a White Russian. All fixed!

2 oz Vodka

**1 oz Coffee-flavored liqueur,
      Kahlua is recommended**

**3 oz Heavy cream
      (less or more, to taste)**

      Ice

Mix the drink: Pour vodka, coffee liqueur, and heavy cream into glass. Stir until all ingredients are fully blended. Add ice. Serve.

MANHATTAN

This cocktail is likely the oldest cocktail mentioned on *Gilmore Girls*. Dating back to the 1800s, it is still a popular beverage today. Still, in over 100 years, Lorelai may be the first and only person to drink hers garnished with eight maraschino cherries.

When you're feeling peckish, take a lesson from Lorelai; you can enjoy this as both a drink and an appetizer, just pile in more cherries.

	Ice
2 oz	Rye whisky
1 oz	Sherry
¼ t	Bitters
1	Maraschino cherry

Mix cocktail: Fill a shaker half with ice. Pour whisky, sherry, and bitters into shaker. Shake until well-blended.

Serve: Stain into a small martini glass. Garnish with a maraschino cherry . . . or eight. Serve.

SHIRLEY TEMPLE

The Queen of the Mocktail—during the first few seasons, this sweet, sweet nonalcoholic drink was reserved strictly for parties at Emily and Richard's, with teenaged Rory drinking most of them. Once Richard had his second heart attack, it was suddenly "mocktails for everyone!" While this may have seemed like a nice gesture—Emily and the girls showing solidarity during Richard's recovery—"Mocktail Hour" only lasted for one episode. After that, everyone, including Richard, got right back into the hooch. Ah . . . the magic healing powers of television.

4 oz	Ginger beer
1 oz	Grenadine
1 oz	Lemon juice, freshly squeezed
	Ice
1	Maraschino cherry, for garnish
1	Lemon wedge, for garnish

Mix and serve: Pour ginger beer into an 8-ounce tumbler or highball glass. Add grenadine and lemon juice. Stir gently, until liquids are combined. Add ice. Garnish with cherry and lemon wedge. Serve.

Booze it up: To turn this into a "Shirley Temple Black" simply add 1 oz White Rum, stir, and serve.

Tester—Melissa McAndrews

HOT CHOCOLATE

TOWN FAVORITE

Taylor's decision to begin serving Hot Chocolate at his soda shop(pe) made it seem like he was stepping over the line into Luke's territory. After all, serving a product which directly competes with one of your landlord's products seems like a bad business decision, doesn't it? But no one cares about that kind of stuff when there are free samples!

You don't have to wait in line for a tiny taste of this stuff—make your own big batch, then enjoy it while spying out the window on your neighbors.

½ c	Semisweet/60%-cacao chocolate chips or bar
½ c	Strongly brewed coffee
1 T	Maple syrup
1½ c	Half-and-half

Prep ingredients: Set aside two 8-ounce coffee mugs or cups. In three separate bowls/cups, measure out chocolate, coffee, and maple syrup. Set aside. (Don't skip this step! You will not have time to measure these once the heating begins.)

Heat ingredients: In medium saucepan, heat half-and-half to a rumbling boil, stirring occasionally with a wire whisk. Watch it closely—just as the milk begins to bubble up and rise to the edge of the pan, add chocolate chips. Whisk until chocolate is melted. Continue whisking until mixture takes on a smooth, creamy consistency. Bring to a boil. Add coffee and maple syrup. Whisk until fully blended. Immediately remove from heat.

Without allowing any time for the chocolate to cool, pour it into coffee mugs/cups. Serve.

Booze it up: Spike this drink by stirring in 1½ ounces of a coffee-flavored liqueur (Kahlua recommended) before pouring into individual cups.

Makes 2 servings.

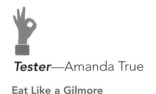

Tester—Amanda True

Eat Like a Gilmore

CHAI LATTE

TOWN FAVORITE

Poor Christopher just never fits in around Stars Hollow, does he? Whether he's having his credit card declined at the book store, or wearing his slick city duds to a man date with a farmer, or killing every ounce of buzz at the Knit-a-thon—when he's there, he's out of his element, and it shows.

Remember early in Season 2, when he ordered a Chai Latte from Luke's? That's the first moment we really saw how out-of-place Christopher can be.

He did get one thing right (besides siring Rory): Chai Lattes are delicious!

3 c	Water
1 T	Minced or grated ginger, peeled
1 t	Cinnamon
1 t	Cardamom
6	Stars anise
¼ t	Nutmeg
¼ t	Allspice
¼ t	Cloves, ground
½ t	Black or pink peppercorns
3 T	Honey
6	Black tea bags
1½ c	Whole milk

Heat spices in water: Pour water into medium saucepan. Add ginger, cinnamon, cardamom, stars anise, nutmeg, allspice, cloves, and peppercorns. Stir until combined. The anise and some of the spices will float on the top—that's okay. Continue stirring every 30 seconds or so. Bring to a boil. Add honey and stir until it is fully dissolved. Remove from heat and add tea bags. Allow the tea to steep in the water for 4 minutes.

Froth and heat milk: Pour milk into a 16-ounce glass jar. Add lid and close tightly. Shake jar vigorously for 1 minute. Remove lid. You'll notice a froth or foam has formed on top of the milk. Place jar in microwave (remember: metal lids do *not* go in the microwave!). Cook on high power for 1 minute.

Assemble Chai Latte: Strain spiced tea through a fine strainer, directly into a mug or coffee cup until it is ⅔-full. Fill the remaining ⅓ with milk. Spoon foam onto top, if desired. Serve.

WASSAIL

SOOKIE'S KITCHEN

"The Bracebridge Dinner" episode is the favorite *Gilmore Girls* episode for many people. It definitely ranks in my Top 3. It would probably reach #1 if Rune wasn't in it. It gave us a Björk snowwoman, surprise horse-drawn-sleigh rides, Mrs. Kim's seminar on how to pack for an overnight trip, tips on how to look Stella McCartney fashionable on a Walmart budget, and lots of unfamiliar food.

This is the drink Sookie served that evening: a traditional spiked apple cider. "Wassail," as it is known, may also be used as a verb; "to go wassailing" means to have a ceremony in the orchard (often on New Year's Eve), to recite a traditional chant, and then sing to the trees while pouring the wassail onto the roots. This ritual is thought to bring good luck to the harvest in the coming year.

The ancient term "wassail" means "Be in good health." May this winter drink find you in good health and bring you good fortune in the year ahead!

10	Red apples, quartered
	Water
2 T	Whole cloves
2 T	Allspice berries
2 T	Freshly sliced ginger
8	Cinnamon sticks
2	Nutmegs, whole, lightly grated around the outside
1 T	Peppercorns, black, pink, or assorted
1 c	Orange juice, freshly squeezed
¼ c	Lemon juice, freshly squeezed
1 c	Brandy
3 T	Honey
8	Additional cinnamon sticks, for garnish
1	Orange, thinly sliced into 8 rounds, for garnish

Spice and boil apples: Fill Dutch oven with the quartered apples. Add just enough water to fully cover the apples. Add cloves, allspice, ginger, cinnamon sticks, nutmegs, and peppercorns. Stir together. Bring to a boil over high heat. Reduce heat and continue to boil for 1 hour.

Mash the apples: Using a slotted spoon, remove the apples and place them in a large mixing bowl. Using a potato masher or a hand mixer, mash the apples until all are a mealy consistency. Return them to the spiced water and continue to boil for 30 minutes.

Make the apple cider: Place a fine strainer into a large bowl. Using a ladle, begin ladling the apple mixture into the strainer—one or two cups at a time. Use the rounded cup part of the ladle to press the apples against the strainer—this will extract the remaining juice. Once all juice has been extracted from that batch, discard the remaining apple bits, and start again with two more ladles' full. Continue until all of the apple mixture has been strained. The liquid in the bowl is your apple cider.

Make the Wassail: Return the juice/apple cider to the Dutch oven and continue heating over medium heat. Do not allow the juice to boil. Stir in the orange juice, lemon juice, and brandy. Once the liquid is hot, stir in the honey until it is fully blended into the liquid.

Serve: Ladle into punch, coffee, or tea cups. Garnish each with a cinnamon stick and a thin slice of orange. Serve.

Makes approximately 8 cups.

Pancakes, French Toast,
Omelets & Cereals

PANCAKES

Well, here it is, the fluffy foundation of breakfast at Luke's: pancakes. If coffee is the star of Luke's morning show, then the pancake is its trusty sidekick. Forget what the "Breakfast Special" sign says—coffee's costar is pancakes. What's more—pancakes adapt to any mood:

- Suffering from a bad breakup? Add chocolate chips & whipped cream.
- Celebrating your engagement? Add blueberries, free of charge!
- Heading off to college? Wrap a pancake around a sausage, tie it with a strip of bacon, and do your going-to-college walk all the way to New Haven.

So whether you're wallowing, celebrating, or marking a major milestone, Luke's pancakes are here for you. Enjoy!

2 c	Flour
4 t	Baking powder
1½ t	Salt
2	Eggs
2 T	Sugar
2 c	Buttermilk
⅓ c	Whole milk
2 T	Butter, melted
	Vegetable oil, for frying

Optional Add-ins:

¾ c	Blueberries
¾ c	Chocolate chips

Prep oven: Preheat oven to 200°F and position a cookie sheet or oven-safe plate on center rack with at least 3 inches clearance above it.

Mix dry ingredients: In medium bowl, mix flour, baking powder, and salt. Set aside.

Mix wet ingredients: In large mixing bowl, add eggs and whisk until smooth. Add sugar and buttermilk. Whisk to combine.

Make batter: Pour dry ingredients into wet ingredients—whisk to combine. Add milk. Whisk. Add butter. Whisk. This is the batter. Fold in any add-ins.

Fry pancakes: Coat a large frying pan with 1 tablespoon vegetable oil. Over medium-high heat, allow the oil to warm up for 2–3 minutes. Pour ½ cup of batter into pan. Use pan's handle to angle pan back and forth until batter is spread evenly. Fry pancake for 2–3 minutes; once the center begins to bubble, flip the pancake. Once you see the pancake puff up/rise in the pan, fry for another 60–90 seconds. Remove pancake and place it on plate in oven to keep it warm. Repeat until all batter has been fried. Serve with butter and maple syrup.

Makes 8–10 pancakes.

Tester—Emily Moeller

PUMPKIN PANCAKES

No show does "autumn" better than *Gilmore Girls*—the clothing, the decorations, the town events. It seems like once the first leaf falls, every last townsperson gets into the spirit—even Luke. While he's not much for foofy décor, he seems perfectly comfortable expressing his fall inspiration in the form of food. Namely, Pumpkin Pancakes. Pair these with the Cinnamon Butter on page 111, and you'll be just as happy as Luke (without having to hire Froggy!).

2 c	Flour
2 t	Baking powder
1 t	Baking soda
1 t	Cinnamon, ground
½ t	Nutmeg, ground
½ t	Cloves, ground
½ t	Salt
1	Egg
1½ c	Buttermilk
3 T	Brown sugar
1 t	Vanilla
1⅓ c	Pumpkin, cooked or canned
2 T	Butter, melted
	Vegetable oil, for frying

Prep oven: Preheat oven to 200°F and position a cookie sheet or oven-safe plate on center rack with at least 3 inches clearance above it.

Mix dry ingredients: In medium bowl, mix flour, baking powder, baking soda, cinnamon, nutmeg, cloves, and salt. Set aside.

Mix wet ingredients: In large mixing bowl, add egg, and whisk until smooth. Add buttermilk, brown sugar, and vanilla. Whisk to combine.

Make batter: Pour dry ingredients into wet ingredients—whisk to combine. Add pumpkin. Whisk. Add butter. Whisk. This is the batter.

Fry pancakes: Coat a large frying pan with 1 tablespoon vegetable oil. Over medium-high heat, allow the oil to warm up for 2–3 minutes. Pour ½ cup of batter into pan. Use pan's handle to angle pan back and forth until batter is spread evenly. Fry pancake for 2–3 minutes; once the very center begins to bubble, wait 30 seconds then flip the pancake. Once you see the pancake puff up/rise in the pan, fry for another 60–90 seconds. Remove pancake and place it on plate in oven to keep it warm. Repeat until all batter has been fried. Serve with butter and maple syrup.

Makes 8–10 pancakes.

Tester—Emily Moeller

3-EGG OMELET

Michel must have willpower of steel—because when Sookie presented this omelet to him and he refused it, cries were heard around the world. When Sookie creates a 3-Egg Omelet made with pancetta and goat cheese, cooked in a sherry olive oil, just for you—you eat it. Period!

3	Eggs
½ c	Cubed pancetta
1 T	Olive oil
1 T	Sherry
¼ t	Black pepper
¼ t	Kosher salt
3 T	Goat cheese
	Chopped fresh parsley, for garnish

Whip eggs: In a medium bowl, use a whisk or fork to whip the eggs. Set aside.

Fry pancetta: Place a paper towel on a large plate. Set aside. In a large frying pan, fry the pancetta over medium-high heat until the edges are lightly browned. Using a slotted spoon, remove the pancetta to the paper towel.

Make omelet: Combine oil and sherry in a large frying pan over medium-high heat. Allow liquids to heat for 2 minutes. Add egg. Use the handle of the pan to angle pan so egg evenly covers the bottom. Cook for 20–30 seconds. Sprinkle pepper and salt evenly over egg. As egg cooks, add pancetta and goat cheese, distributing both evenly across egg.

Fold omelet and serve: Gently tuck a spatula under one side of the omelet. Lift that side and fold it over the top—so the omelet is folded in half. Slide the omelet onto a plate. Garnish with fresh parsley. Serve.

Makes 1 omelet.

CHILAQUILES

With Luke away, Caesar seized the opportunity to inject some of his Mexican heritage into the breakfast menu. He served up authentic Chilaquiles to Luke's customers. Instantly, they were hooked! I can see why. If you like Mexican food, this will add that same spicy, crunchy goodness to your first meal of the day. You may even find yourself enthusiastically yelling "CHILAQUILES!" after the first bite!

20	Corn tortillas
1½ c	Vegetable oil
1	Medium yellow onion, coarsely chopped
10 oz	Red chile sauce, canned
¾ c	Water
½ c	Queso fresco, crumbled (may substitute with Monterey Jack cheese, shredded)
½ c	Chopped cilantro, divided
½ t	Salt
2 T	Olive oil, divided
8	Eggs
	Salt & pepper
	Crema Mexicana, optional
	Additional chopped cilantro, for garnish

Cook tortillas and onions in oil: Lay out wire racks with paper towels underneath them (this is where the tortillas will drain excess oil). Stack the tortillas. Use a sharp knife to cut them like a pizza: two cuts in the shape of a plus sign, two cuts in the shape of an X. The result will be 160 little tortilla triangles. Heat oil in Dutch oven. Use a candy thermometer to measure the temperature of the oil. When it hits 360°–380°F, carefully add in the tortilla pieces and the onion. Stir gently to coat the tortilla pieces evenly with oil. Turn the chips every 2 minutes until most are crispy. Use a slotted spoon to move the tortilla chips and onion from the oil to the wire racks. Discard the remaining oil from the pot (be careful—oil will be hot!).

Cook the Chilaquiles: In the same Dutch oven, add the red chile sauce and water. Stir to combine and bring to a boil over high heat. Add the chips and onions to the sauce and gently coat the chips with the sauce. Add the cheese, cilantro, and salt. Gently stir. Spoon Chilaquiles in equal portions onto 8 plates.

Cook the eggs: Place large fry pan on a burner over medium heat. Add 1 tablespoon olive oil to coat the bottom of the pan. Crack 4 eggs into pan, leaving as much space as possible between each egg. Cook until egg whites turn from translucent to solid white. Using a spatula, gently turn each egg over. Season each egg with a pinch of salt and pepper. Cook for 90 seconds, or until whites are no longer runny (yolks will still be runny).

Assemble and serve: Place one egg each on top of 4 portions of Chilaquiles. Repeat process for next 4 eggs. Drizzle crema Mexicana across top of each plate, if desired. Garnish with cilantro. Serve.

Makes 8 servings.

FRENCH TOAST

Even though Jason did make this for Lorelai the morning after he dropped his "here's a key to my apartment" bomb on her, this recipe is attributed to Luke's Diner. Why? Because it's a popular, if subtle, behind-the-scenes player on the diner's breakfast menu. Many times it's ordered and enjoyed, especially by Rory, without a lot of fanfare. So, should Jason making it one time usurp Luke, who consistently served up quality French Toast for seven seasons? I don't think so.

That said—there's nothing stopping you from taking it to-go. Simply put it into a baggie, together with some bacon, and pour syrup on top. This way you can eat it on your way to the inn.

Please drive safely.

2	Eggs
¼ c	Milk
½ t	Vanilla
1 T	Olive oil
4	Bread slices (white, egg, or cinnamon) or 2 croissants, cut in half
	Butter, for serving
	Maple syrup, for serving

Mix egg batter: Crack eggs into shallow bowl. Using a whisk or fork, vigorously mix the eggs until yolks and whites are completely combined. Add milk and vanilla and continue mixing until combined.

Heat oil: In a large frying pan, heat oil over medium-high heat for 2 minutes.

Make French Toast: One at a time, dip 2 pieces of bread or both halves of one croissant into egg batter, turning once, so each side is fully coated. Hold the battered piece over the bowl for a few seconds so excess batter can drip off. Place the pieces in the frying pan. Cook for 2 minutes. Use a spatula to flip both pieces. Cook the other side for 1–2 minutes, until bread is golden brown and not mushy. Remove from pan and place on a plate. Repeat with the remaining bread/croissant.

Serve with butter and maple syrup.

Makes 2 servings.

EGG WHITE OMELET

SOOKIE'S KITCHEN

Presenting the breakfast of super-low-rise-jeans champions—the Egg White Omelet, just as Michel specified.

This really is a nutritious, easy dish to whip up (without any blueberries to count!). It's the perfect breakfast to serve the morning after a *Cop Rock*–marathon binge.

½ t   Olive oil

1 t   Water

½ c   Egg whites
           (about 3 large eggs)

1 t   Minced chives

¼ t   Black pepper

1   Roma tomato, diced

½ c   Finely chopped white
            or cremini mushrooms

           Chopped fresh parsley or
              chives, for garnish

Make omelet: Combine oil and water in a large frying pan over medium-high heat. Allow liquids to heat for 2 minutes. Add egg whites. Use the handle of the pan to angle pan so egg whites cover the bottom evenly. Cook for 20–30 seconds. Sprinkle chives and black pepper evenly over egg whites. As egg cooks, add tomato and mushrooms, distributing both evenly.

Fold omelet and serve: Gently tuck a spatula under one side of the omelet. Lift that side and fold it over the top, so the omelet is folded in half. Slide the omelet onto a plate. Garnish with fresh parsley or chives. Serve.

Makes 1 omelet.

DONUTS

If there's any food Luke uses to show his love, appreciation, and devotion to Lorelai—it's donuts. Donuts seem like one of the very last foods Luke, himself, would choose to eat. They're sugary with zero nutritional value. But Lorelai loves donuts; especially on Tuesday Sprinkle Day. So every instance when we see Luke give Lorelai a donut, especially if the two are feuding at the time and she's using a pseudonym, the gesture is an expression of his underlying love.

Here's your chance to express your feelings for someone special (or for yourself)—make these donuts, dress them up with sprinkles any day of the week, and give them away like the sweet little love notes they are.

2 pkgs	Active dry yeast
1 c	Milk
3 T	Water
¼ c	Sugar
4 c	Flour
½ t	Salt
½ c	Shortening, melted
2	Eggs
4 c	Shortening, for frying

Vanilla Glaze:

2 c	Confectioners' sugar
2 T	Butter, melted and cooled
3 T	Milk
1 t	Vanilla

Pink Strawberry Glaze:

2 c	Confectioners' sugar
1 T	Butter, melted and cooled
2 t	Imitation strawberry extract
3–4 T	Milk

Chocolate Glaze:

1½ c	Confectioners' sugar
½ c	Unsweetened baking cocoa
2 T	Butter, melted and cooled
4–5 T	Milk

Proof the yeast: Pour yeast into a large mixing bowl and set aside. Combine milk and water in a medium saucepan over medium-high heat. Insert a candy thermometer and heat liquid to 110°–120°F only. Add sugar and stir to dissolve. Pour mixture onto the yeast, without stirring. Let sit for 5–10 minutes.

Combine dry ingredients: In a medium bowl, combine flour and salt. Stir to evenly distribute salt. Set aside.

Combine wet ingredients: In a small bowl, combine the shortening and the eggs—if the shortening is still warm, take care to whisk the eggs quickly so they don't partially cook in the shortening. Add to the bowl with the yeast and, with a hand mixer, beat on a medium-low setting until fully combined.

Make dough: Add about ⅓ of the flour mixture to the wet ingredients. Set hand mixer to medium-low and begin to mix. As flour gets incorporated, gradually add more flour, scraping down the sides of the bowl in between additions. Once all flour has been incorporated, stop mixing. Avoid over-mixing. Dough should be slightly tacky to the touch. If it isn't, add 1–2 tablespoons water and use hand mixer to mix again—only until the water is blended into the dough.

Knead dough: Turn dough out onto a floured work surface. Knead for 25–30 turns.

Allow dough to rise: Grease the inside of a large mixing bowl. Place dough inside and cover with a clean dish towel. Place bowl in a warm location and let rise for 60–90 minutes.

Cut donuts: Once dough has doubled in size (at least)—punch it down and turn it onto a floured work surface. Using a rolling pin, roll out dough until it's about 1-inch thick. Use a donut cutter or a 3½ inch–diameter glass for the outside plus a 1-inch diameter plastic water or soda bottle to cut out the middle of the donuts. Place donuts on a cookie sheet covered with parchment paper. Cover with a clean towel and allow donuts to rise for another 30–40 minutes.

Make glaze: Add the confectioners' sugar to a shallow bowl. Stir in the other ingredients until smooth. Remove any lumps by smashing them with the backside of a spoon. If there are many lumps, push the glaze through a strainer. Set aside.

Fry donuts: Place 4 cups shortening in a Dutch oven; melt over high heat. Heat to 360°F (use candy thermometer). Fry donuts 2 at a time in melted shortening. Fry for 1 minute per side or until the dough turns golden brown. Use tongs, a long fork, or chopsticks to flip the donut. Once finished, pull the donuts from the oil using tongs or a slotted spoon. Hold each donut over the oil for a few seconds so any excess shortening drips off. Place donuts on cooling rack.

Glaze donuts: Dip each donut, face-down, halfway into the glaze. Pull the donut out. For a fully glazed donut, flip it around, and dip the other side. Pull the donut from the glaze and hold it over the bowl for a few seconds so excess glaze drips off. Place on a cooling rack. Add sprinkles while glaze is still wet. Allow donuts to set for 10 minutes. Serve.

Note: *The way to get glaze smooth and even on donuts is to glaze them while they are still hot. If you make the glaze(s) while the donuts are rising — you'll be ready to glaze when the donuts come out of the fryer!*

BANANAS FOSTER FRENCH TOAST

So your inn just burned down. Take solace—because now you get to have a decadent breakfast, perhaps the best of your life, made by Sookie St. James in the comfort of Luke's Diner. How's that for a silver lining?

What makes this dish so delicious? Maybe it's the part where you light it on fire. No seriously. Someone on the writing team loves irony.

	French Toast from page 51, using croissants
2 T	Butter
4 T	Brown sugar
1 T	Maple syrup
1½ t	Molasses
¼ c	Spiced rum
¼ c	Half-and-half
2	Bananas, halved lengthwise and across the middle
	Whipped cream, for serving, optional

Make caramel sauce: Melt butter in medium frying pan. Add brown sugar, maple syrup, and molasses. Stir until fully dissolved and mixture takes on a smooth, dark, caramel syrup consistency. Add rum. Using a long match or a long-handled lighter, carefully light the rum on fire. Stand back until the rum has burned off. The flame will extinguish itself.

Make bananas foster: Add half-and-half to frying pan. Stir until blended. Add bananas. Reduce heat to low. Cook bananas for 2–3 minutes, turning once. Spoon banana pieces onto the French Toast. Spoon sauce over the top. Add whipped cream. Serve.

Makes 2 servings.

CAJUN EGGS BENEDICT

As great as Sookie's cooking is, her people skills are questionable, especially when it comes to food prep. She doesn't trust her own trained staff to make sauces. She hovers over Jackson when he cooks romantic dinners for her. When Luke isn't looking, she adds ingredients to plates as they come out of the diner's kitchen; then tells his customers they'll like the food better her way. She is a beloved soul, but when it comes to cooking, Sookie's passion for perfection can be annoying. So imagine Luke accidentally dropping cayenne pepper into her hollandaise sauce—she must have wigged out! No one knows how they got past that faux pas, but they did. In fact, that "accident" was the catalyst to Sookie and Luke working together to create this dish.

Against all Stars Hollow odds, here it is—a Sookie/Luke creation!

2	English muffins
2	Andouille sausages
	Water
2 T	White vinegar
4	Eggs

Cajun Sauce:

	Water
2	Egg yolks
4 t	Lemon juice, freshly squeezed
½ t	Kosher salt
¼ t	Black pepper
½ t	Thyme, dried
¼ t	Cayenne
1 t	Chili powder
1 T	Spanish paprika
1 stick	Butter, melted

Prep English muffins and sausages: In a toaster, toast English muffins to a golden brown. Place them on 2 plates, 1 muffin per plate, nooks and crannies–side up. Split sausages down the middle lengthwise, cut them in half across the middle and place in a small frying pan, over medium-high heat. Cook for 3–4 minutes, until edges become browned. Flip and cook for an additional 3 minutes. Remove from pan and position 2 pieces of sausage on each English muffin half. Set aside.

Poach eggs: Fill a medium saucepan half-full with water. Over medium-high heat, bring water to a boil. Add vinegar and stir. Crack 1 egg into a coffee cup. Position the cup so it is just above the water, but not touching the water. Slowly and gently turn the egg out of the cup and into the water. Cook for 3 minutes. Using a slotted spoon, remove the egg from the water and place it atop the sausage on one of the English muffin halves. Repeat for the 3 remaining eggs.

Make the sauce: Fill a small saucepan with 2 inches of water. Place a larger bowl on top of the saucepan, making sure the bottom of the bowl doesn't touch the water. Add the yolks, lemon juice, and spices to the bowl. Whisk until all ingredients are fully combined. Move the bowl to a countertop. Using a hand mixer, begin mixing the sauce on low speed. Continue mixing while slowly drizzling the butter into the sauce. The butter will emulsify the sauce.

Serve: Pour the sauce over the tops of the egg-sausage-muffin stacks. Serve.

Makes 2 servings.

CEREAL COMBOS

Cereal, one of the four food pillars of college life, made several appearances at Yale. Its spotlight moment, however, took place when Paris revealed the Cereal Combo to Rory (who later passed it on to Lorelai). The Cereal Combo is a great way to add some sparkle to a humdrum cereal routine. Combining a healthy cereal with one or two sugary cereals creates the best of both worlds—nutrition and fun!

In addition to "The Bulldog"—which is Paris's original recipe—below are five more suggested combinations. Take these combos as inspiration, a jumping off point—experiment and find your own favorite combos. Create your signature combo! Or just revel in the feeling of power you get when you open multiple cereal boxes at once.

The Bulldog

½ c	Cap'n Crunch®
½ c	Rice Krispies®
½ c	Frosted Mini Wheats®

The Gluten-Free

½ c	Multi Grain Cheerios®
½ c	Trix®
½ c	Honey Nut Chex™

Chocolate Peanut Butter Crunch

¾ c	Cocoa Puffs®
¾ c	Cap'n Crunch's Peanut Butter Crunch®

Flaky Trix Mix

½ c	Frosted Flakes™
½ c	Trix®
½ c	Corn Flakes®

K-Pop Crunch

½ c	Cinnamon Toast Crunch®
½ c	Special K® Protein
½ c	Corn Pops®

The Kix-Starter

½ c	Honey Nut Cheerios®
½ c	Cinnamon Life®
½ c	Kix®

Pour cereals into bowl. Add ½–1 cup milk. Serve.

COFFEE CAKE

On the morning of Rory's sixteenth, birthday Luke shows us, for the first time, a glimpse of his softer side. When she and Lane arrive at the diner before school, Luke has a table set up with balloons and this cake—just waiting for the birthday girl to arrive, so he could start her day off in a special way.

If you'd like to show someone your softer side, surprise them with this cake. Just be sure to remember the coffee!

2 c	Flour
¾ c	Sugar
1 T	Baking powder
½ t	Salt
1	Egg
¾ c	Sour cream
½ c	Half-and-half
1½ t	Vanilla
½ c	Butter, cold

Streusel Topping:

½ c	Flour
½ c	Sugar
¾ c	Brown sugar
1 T	Cinnamon
¼ c	Butter

Prep oven and pan: Place oven rack in center position. Preheat oven to 350°F. Grease and flour an 8x8-inch baking pan. Set aside.

Combine dry ingredients: In a medium bowl, combine flour, sugar, baking powder, and salt. Set aside.

Combine wet ingredients: In a large mixing bowl, beat egg until yolk and whites are fully combined. Stir in sour cream, half-and-half, and vanilla.

Make batter: Using a large fork, mix dry ingredients into wet ingredients. Stir to combine, but no more than that. Cut in butter. Pour batter into prepared pan. Set aside.

Make Streusel Topping: In a medium bowl, mix flour, sugar, brown sugar, and cinnamon. Cut in butter until little brown balls start to form. Spread streusel evenly across the top of the batter.

Bake Coffee Cake: Place pan in oven. Bake for 25–30 minutes. Insert a toothpick to test doneness. When it comes out clean, cake is done. Remove from oven. Cool for 10 minutes. Cut and serve.

Muffins, Rolls, Breads & Scones

SCONES

Scones are mentioned in many episodes of *Gilmore Girls*—though I'm not sure we ever actually see a scone. Still, everyone's talking about them—from the folks at the Cheshire Cat bed and breakfast, to Emily and Richard raving about scone mix, to Logan rating scone dryness during his London stint. Through it all, only one person's scones were mentioned on two separate occasions, being described as both "magical" and "heavenly"—Sookie's scones.

Scones are designed to be dry, neutral-tasting quick breads—nuggets of flaky goodness you can make in a jiff, then pop open and smear with butter, jam, clotted cream, or all three. This recipe produces a more flavorful scone because it's fashioned after Sookie's baking sensibilities, yet it still qualifies as simple and traditional. If you want to experiment with add-ins like chocolate chips, cranberries, or red currants—go for it! But, if you're more of a purist, you're covered. These little dream bites are designed to taste great just as they are.

Put aside those insurance papers, pour yourself a nice cuppa, and let a scone transport you to tea time in Sookie's kitchen.

2 c	Flour, plus more for baking
⅓ c	Granulated sugar
1 t	Baking powder
1 t	Baking soda
¼ t	Salt
1 stick	Butter, cold
1	Large egg
½ c	Mascarpone (Italian cream cheese)
1 T	Lemon juice, freshly squeezed
½ c	Coarse sugar

Prepare oven and pan: Place oven rack in center of oven. Preheat oven to 375°F. Coat the bottom of a cookie sheet with 1–2 tablespoons of flour. Set aside.

Combine dry ingredients: In a medium mixing bowl, combine flour, sugar, baking powder, baking soda, and salt.

Cut in butter—with a pastry blender: Place the butter in the bowl with the dry ingredients and use the pastry blender to "cut in" the butter until there are no big chunks of butter.

Without a pastry blender: Either cut the stick of butter into 15 or more very thin slices or grate the butter on a block grater. Then add butter into the bowl with the dry ingredients. Then use a knife or fork to cut in the butter.

Blend wet ingredients: In a small mixing bowl, beat the egg until the yolk and whites are fully combined. Add marscarpone and lemon juice. Beat on low speed with a hand mixer until fully blended (it's okay if there are a few small lumps of marscarpone).

Make the dough: Pour the wet mixture into the dry ingredients. With a fork, begin to work in the liquid. At first, it will seem like there is not nearly enough liquid for all of the dry ingredients, but after about a dozen strokes, you'll see a dough beginning to form. Continue to mix the dough with the fork, until there is no loose, dry flour at the bottom of the bowl.

Cut the Scones: Cover a 12x12-inch square work surface with a light layer of flour. Turn out the dough onto the floured surface. Using your hands, shape the dough into a rough circle. The dough should be about ½-inch thick. Use a round cookie cutter to make round scones. Or use a large knife or pizza cutter to make triangular scones. Place the scones onto the prepared cookie sheet, leaving at least ½ inch between each. Top each scone with ½ teaspoon coarse sugar.

Bake Scones and serve: Place cookie sheet on center rack. Bake for 15 minutes. When the bottom edges turn golden brown, and the tops look light golden brown, the scones are done. Remove from oven. Let cool for 2 minutes. Serve with butter, clotted cream, and/or fresh preserves.

Makes 10–12 triangles or 14–16 (2-inch diameter) rounds.

Tester—Brianne Wetzel

Eat Like a Gilmore

ORANGE-GLAZED MUFFINS

Sookie used these muffins as a bribe to talk Lorelai into letting Rune live at the inn. Yes, Rune—Jackson's rude, mean-spirited cousin who ruthlessly insulted Lorelai throughout their "date." Yet, Sookie still got a "yes." Not only did he get to stay, Rune also got hired as the inn's handyman and got to live in Rory's first home—the potting shed. Either Lorelai has a secret soft spot for Rune, or these muffins have invisible, magical powers.

It's the latter. This muffin, with its fresh, moist citrus flavor, is enticing enough on its own. But once it's covered in the gooey, sweet orange glaze—it really does become magical.

	Cooking spray or oil
2 c	Flour
½ c	Brown sugar
¼ t	Salt
½ t	Baking soda
2 t	Baking powder
⅓ c	Orange juice, freshly squeezed
1	Egg
⅓ c	Olive oil
⅔ c	Sour cream
1 T	Orange zest
1 t	Vanilla

Orange Glaze:

	1½ c Confectioners' sugar
3 T	Orange juice, freshly squeezed

Prep oven and baking pan: Move oven rack to the center position and preheat oven to 400°F. Coat jumbo muffin tin with cooking spray or oil. Set aside.

Combine dry ingredients: In a small mixing bowl, combine flour, brown sugar, salt, and baking soda. Set aside.

Combine wet ingredients: In a small bowl, mix together the baking powder with orange juice to create a foam reaction. In a separate mixing bowl, lightly whisk the egg, and then add olive oil, sour cream, orange zest, and vanilla. Mix in the orange juice–baking powder combination. Combine with a fork until smooth.

Mix batter: Add dry ingredients to wet ingredients and mix with fork until fully combined. Take care not to over-mix.

Bake muffins: Pour batter into prepared muffin pan. Fill each muffin cup until it's nearly full. Bake muffins for 20 minutes. Remove from oven and let stand for 10 minutes. Remove muffins from pan and place on wire rack(s). Let cool.

Glaze muffins: In a shallow bowl, mix together the confectioners' sugar and orange juice until it forms a translucent, orangish-white liquid. Dip each muffin, top-down, into the glaze. Turn the muffins right side up and let them set for a few minutes until the glaze hardens. Serve.

Make muffin tops/muffin bottoms: Allow muffins to cool completely. Slice off muffin tops. Save muffin bottoms for Muffin Bottom & Pudding Pie (see page 215).

Makes 6 jumbo muffins/muffin tops.

APPLE SPICE MUFFINS

CONTRIBUTED BY SHEHZEEN AHMED & MEHREEN AHMED

Remember the morning in Season 7 when Lorelai opened the door and Sookie was there carrying a basket of muffins? Well, technically it was muffin tops. She'd baked four types of muffins in an effort to bribe Lorelai to babysit for Martha and Davy. This is the first of those four recipes. Make them all; then choose your favorite! If you prefer to eat only the tops, à la Lorelai, then put on your magic socks, give them a few kicks, and you'll find yourself on page 215, turning the bottoms into a pie!

	Cooking spray or oil
½ c	Butter, softened
¾ c	Granulated sugar
2	Eggs
⅓ c	Milk
2 t	Baking powder
pinch	Salt
1 t	Ground cinnamon
1 t	Ground allspice
1½ c	Flour
2 c	Peeled and chopped apples

Streusel Topping:

¼ c	Butter, softened
½ c	Light brown sugar
¼ c	Flour
1½ t	Ground cinnamon

Prep oven and pan: Preheat oven to 375°F. Coat jumbo muffin tin with cooking spray or oil.

Combine wet ingredients: In a bowl, mix together butter and sugar. Whisk in eggs and milk until smooth.

Combine dry ingredients: In a separate bowl, combine baking powder, salt, cinnamon, allspice, and flour.

Mix batter: Add dry ingredient mixture to wet ingredient mixture. Fold in chopped apples.

Bake muffins: Pour batter into muffin cups until they are almost full. For the Streusel Topping, mix all ingredients until crumbly. Sprinkle over the top of each muffin. Bake for 20 minutes at 375°F.

Serve: Remove from oven and let cool, in the pan, for 10 minutes. Move muffins from the pan to wire racks and let cool. Serve.

Make muffin tops/muffin bottoms: Let cool completely and slice off muffin tops. Save muffin bottoms for Muffin Bottom & Pudding Pie (see page 215).

Makes 6 jumbo muffins/muffin tops.

Notes: *We used Granny Smith apples, but other sweet and crisp apples can be used! The Streusel Topping can also be used on the Apple Cinnamon Walnut Muffins on page 75.*

LEMON POPPY SEED MUFFINS

CONTRIBUTED BY SHEHZEEN AHMED & MEHREEN AHMED

Even though a Lemon Poppy Seed Muffin may seem like a predictable, everyday, somewhat humdrum choice—Sookie doesn't really do humdrum (unless she's got a rare case of ennui). Where's the trust?

This is not your average "stand-in-line Monday morning" muffin. This is a "brunch on the veranda" version of an old favorite. So pour yourself a mimosa and turn on some Vivaldi; then sit back and enjoy one of these little glazed breakfast cakes.

	Cooking spray or oil
2 t	Baking powder
3 T	Lemon juice, freshly squeezed
2	Eggs
2 T	Lemon zest
½ c	Butter, softened
1 c	Plain yogurt
¼ t	Salt
½ c	Granulated sugar
2 c	Flour
1 t	Baking soda
⅛ c	Poppy seeds

Icing:

1½ c	Confectioners' sugar
3 T	Lemon juice, freshly squeezed

Prep oven and pan: Preheat oven to 350°F. Coat jumbo muffin tin with cooking spray or oil.

Combine wet ingredients: In a small bowl, mix together the baking powder with lemon juice to create a foam reaction. In a separate bowl, combine eggs, lemon zest, butter, and yogurt. Mix in the lemon juice-baking powder combination.

Combine dry ingredients: Combine salt, sugar, flour, baking soda, and poppy seeds. Add dry ingredient mixture to wet ingredient mixture. Mix until fully combined.

Bake muffins: Pour batter into muffin cups until they are almost full. Bake for 20–23 minutes. Remove from oven. Let muffins cool in the pan for 10 minutes. Remove muffins from pan and cool them on wire racks.

Ice muffins and serve: For the icing, whisk together confectioners' sugar and lemon juice and drizzle over muffin tops. Serve.

Make muffin tops/muffin bottoms: Let cool completely and slice off muffin tops. Save muffin bottoms for Muffin Bottom & Pudding Pie (see page 215).

Makes 6 jumbo muffins/muffin tops.

Notes: *Mixing baking powder and lemon juice will help the muffins to become extra airy and fluffy, and it will also help them rise for larger muffin tops!*

APPLE CINNAMON WALNUT MUFFINS

CONTRIBUTED BY SHEHZEEN AHMED & MEHREEN AHMED

It's a bit of a mystery why Sookie made two types of apple muffins to take to Lorelai's on the same day. I mean, it was the end of January; not really apple season. Was she out of ideas? Was she in a rush? Was she a little off her game due to her soon-to-be-discovered pregnancy? Or, does Jackson's hydroponic greenhouse make it apple season at their house all year 'round?

No matter what caused the apple muffin encore, we're certainly not complaining. When a kitchen maestro like Sookie brings you homemade muffins, you eat them and say "Thank you" and "Please, may I have another?"

	Cooking spray or oil
½ c	Butter, softened
1 t	Vanilla
1 c	Granulated sugar
¼ c	Light brown sugar
2	Eggs
1½ c	Flour, divided
2 t	Baking powder
½ t	Baking soda
pinch	Salt
1 t	Ground cinnamon
1 c	Applesauce
1 c	Coarsely chopped walnuts

Prep oven and pan: Preheat oven to 375°F. Coat jumbo muffin tin with cooking spray or oil.

Combine butter, sugars, and wet ingredients: In a bowl, mix together butter, vanilla, sugar, and light brown sugar. Whisk in eggs until smooth.

Combine dry ingredients: In a separate bowl, combine ½ cup of flour, baking powder, baking soda, salt, and cinnamon.

Mix batter: Add dry ingredient mixture to wet ingredient mixture. Add applesauce, and then slowly mix in remaining 1 cup of flour. Fold in chopped walnuts.

Bake muffins: Pour batter into muffin cups until they are almost full. Bake for 25 minutes.

Cool and serve: Let cool in baking tin for 10 minutes. Then place muffins on wire racks to cool entirely. Serve.

Make muffin tops/muffin bottoms: Let cool completely and slice off muffin tops. Save muffin bottoms for Muffin Bottom & Pudding Pie (see page 215).

Makes 6 jumbo muffins/muffin tops.

DOUBLE CHOCOLATE CHIP MUFFINS

CONTRIBUTED BY SHEHZEEN AHMED & MEHREEN AHMED

Sookie was right about these: they are like a cake—a rich and chocolaty cake. But they're also quick and easy to bake, like a muffin. The perfect combination!

These muffins, along with the coffee Sookie brought from Luke's, made up the very last meal Lorelai and Christopher would ever share as a married couple. About an hour after breakfast is when he found the letter/character reference she wrote for Luke, and over the course of the next day or two, their entire marriage unraveled.

So, in addition to being rich, chocolaty, and easy to make, they also saved Lorelai from a lifetime of being married to the wrong guy. Now that's a muffin.

	Cooking spray or oil
2 c	Flour
1 c	Sugar
½ c	Cocoa powder
½ t	Baking soda
2 t	Baking powder
¼ t	Salt
1 t	Vanilla
1	Egg
½ c	Whole milk
½ c	Olive oil
1 c	Sour cream
1 c	Chocolate chips

Prep oven and baking pan: Preheat oven to 400°F. Coat a jumbo muffin tin with cooking spray or oil.

Combine dry ingredients: In a bowl, mix together flour, sugar, cocoa powder, baking soda, baking powder, and salt. Set aside.

Combine wet ingredients: In a separate bowl, combine vanilla, egg, milk, oil, and sour cream.

Mix batter: Add dry ingredient mixture to wet ingredient mixture. Fold in chocolate chips.

Bake muffins: Pour batter into muffin cups until they are almost full. Bake at 400°F for 5 minutes, and then lower to 350°F for another 20 minutes. Remove from oven and let cool for 10 minutes. Remove muffins from tin; let cool on wire rack. Serve.

Make muffin tops/muffin bottoms: Allow muffins to cool completely. Slice off muffin tops. Save muffin bottoms for Muffin Bottom & Pudding Pie (see page 215).

Makes 6 jumbo muffins/muffin tops.

BLUEBERRY MUFFINS

Blueberry Muffins are so ever-present in the lives of Lorelai and Rory they could become the foundation for a new drinking game; every time a Gilmore girl orders one, eats one, or walks behind Luke's counter to fetch one for herself, take a drink.

But Gilmores aren't much for drinking games. They're more "eating games"-type people. So whip up a batch of these muffins, then snuggle into the sofa to binge-watch a season or two, and eat a Blueberry Muffin every time Lorelai and Rory do. Don't forget the can of whipped cream!

	Cooking spray or oil
2 c	Flour
1 c	Sugar
½ t	Salt
1½ t	Baking powder
1 t	Baking soda
1	Egg
⅓ c	Olive oil
⅔ c	Sour cream
½ c	Whole milk
6 oz	Blueberries
2 T	Coarse sugar, for sprinkling

Prep oven and baking pan: Move oven rack to the center position and preheat oven to 400°F. Coat jumbo muffin tin with cooking spray or oil. Set aside.

Combine dry ingredients: In a medium mixing bowl, combine flour, sugar, salt, baking powder, and baking soda. Set aside.

Combine wet ingredients: In a separate mixing bowl, lightly whisk the egg, then add olive oil, sour cream, and milk. Combine with a fork until smooth.

Mix batter: Add dry ingredients to wet ingredients and mix with fork until fully combined. Take care not to over-mix. Fold in the blueberries.

Bake muffins: Pour batter into prepared muffin pan. Fill each muffin cup until it's nearly full. Sprinkle each muffin with ½ teaspoon coarse sugar. Bake muffins for 20 minutes. Remove from oven and let stand for 10 minutes. Remove muffins from pan and place on wire rack(s). Let cool. Serve.

Make muffin tops/muffin bottoms: Allow muffins to cool completely. Slice off muffin tops. Save muffin bottoms for Muffin Bottom & Pudding Pie (see page 215).

Makes 6 jumbo muffins/muffin tops.

PARKER HOUSE ROLLS

This is one of Rory's favorite foods—Parker House Rolls.

Part of the fun of making these is watching these cute, perfectly uniform balls of dough as they bake, shoulder to shoulder in the pan like Revolutionary War re-enactors. These rolls have a light, crusty top with a soft middle that's just asking to be pulled apart. Smoosh some Irish butter between two warm halves, take a bite, and you'll forget all about having to move out of the pool house.

	Butter and flour, for preparing pan
1½ c	Milk
1	Egg
2¼ t	Active dry yeast
5 T	Unsalted butter, cubed
3 T	Granulated sugar
4 c	Flour, plus extra for kneading and rolling dough
	Additional butter, for greasing bowl
4 T	Butter, melted, for brushing
2 t	Kosher salt, for sprinkling

Prep oven and pan: Make sure the oven rack is in the center position. Preheat oven to 350°F. Coat a 9x13-inch baking pan with butter and then flour. Set aside.

Heat milk and egg: In a medium saucepan, combine milk and the egg, lightly whisking together until blended. Insert a candy thermometer into pan. Warm the mixture to 100–110°F (no hotter) over medium heat. Remove from heat. Immediately, while the mixture is still in the pot, stir in the yeast. Then transfer the whole thing to a large mixing bowl. Let stand for 5 minutes. The yeast will likely begin to get frothy. (If it doesn't—don't panic. Simply move on to the next step.)

Form dough: Add the cubed butter, sugar, and 4 cups of flour to bowl. Combine the ingredients using a hand mixer on low to medium speed until a scraggly dough forms. Cover a flat work surface with a layer of flour. Turn out the dough onto the work surface and knead dough with your hands for 3–4 minutes.

Let dough rise: Grease a large mixing bowl with butter. Place dough in bowl and cover it with a clean dish towel. Allow dough to sit like this for 90 minutes. In this time, it should rise to double its size, or more. The rising may not occur until closer to the end of the 90 minutes, so keep the faith!

Roll the rolls: One more time, turn the dough out onto a floured work surface. With a rolling pin, roll the dough into a rectangle shape that's about 13-inches long by 9-inches wide. Using a sharp knife or a pizza cutter, cut the dough, lengthwise, into 4 long, equal rows. Then cut each row into 6 pieces. This will give you 24 pieces—each piece roughly the same size. Roll each piece into a ball between your palms. You can take any edges and tuck them into the bottom of the ball. Place the balls into the 9x13-inch pan, spacing the rolls ½-inch apart. (You will wind up with 4 rolls across by 6 rolls length-wise.) Allow rolls to rise 20–30 minutes, until they puff up enough to touch each other.

Bake the rolls: Brush the tops of the rolls with melted butter then place the tray in the oven for 30 minutes. I like to brush the rolls with butter every 10 minutes. The final time, I also sprinkle salt on each roll. The rolls will turn a nice golden brown on the top when they're done. Remove from oven and cool for 10 minutes. Remove rolls from pan, separate, and serve.

Makes 24 rolls.

Tester—Amanda True

Eat Like a Gilmore

CORNBREAD

TOWN FAVORITE

This must be one of Jackson's favorites—because Sookie made it for him as part of her "I'm sorry I (accidentally) cheated on you" dinner. Of course Sookie didn't really cheat on Jackson—she just mildly flirted with her buddy from chef's school, Joe.

Sookie served up so many varied foods during that dinner—and Cornbread complemented each of them. So don't think you need to wait for Chili Night to make this! It pairs well with a wide variety of meat dishes, salads, and soups. For a real treat, serve it with homemade butter and crank up some CCR.

	Butter, for preparing pan
¾ c	Cornmeal
¾ c	Flour
1 t	Baking powder
1 t	Salt
½ c	Butter
½ c	Granulated sugar
2	Eggs
¾ c	Buttermilk
½ c	Monterey Jack cheese, shredded

Prep oven and pan: Move oven rack to center position and preheat oven to 350°F. Butter an 8x8-inch square baking pan. Set aside.

Mix dry ingredients: In a small mixing bowl, combine cornmeal, flour, baking powder, and salt. Set aside.

Make batter: In a medium mixing bowl, cream the butter and sugar together using a hand mixer on medium setting. Add eggs and continue to mix until combined. Add buttermilk and cheese—mix on low speed to avoid splatter. Once combined, add half the dry ingredients. Mix thoroughly. Scrape down sides of the bowl with a rubber spatula. Add the remaining dry ingredients. Mix again until no white flour is visible.

Bake cornbread: Turn batter into prepared baking pan. Use rubber spatula to remove remaining batter from bowl. Bake for 30 minutes. Insert a toothpick into cornbread to make sure it's done (the toothpick will come out clean if it is). Remove from oven. Let cool for 5 minutes. Cut into squares. Serve.

Makes 16 pieces of cornbread.

FOCACCIA BREAD
WITH ROSEMARY &
ROASTED GARLIC

For not dating much, Luke's still pretty good at it. Focaccia Bread was the perfect choice for the romantic dinner he prepared for Lorelai. Considering it's a yeast-based bread, it's relatively quick and simple to make after working all day at the diner. Plus, roasting the garlic must have created an impressive aroma throughout his bachelor pad. It also gave him the option of serving the bread with the meal or as an appetizer, with some olive oil and balsamic vinegar. (Well, we are talking about Lorelai, so it was probably both.)

Keep this one in mind for your next home-cooked dinner date!

6–8	Garlic cloves, peeled, smashed
4 T	Olive oil, divided, plus extra for brushing
2 c	Flour, plus extra for kneading
1 t	Salt
½ t	Sugar
¼ t	Black pepper
1 T	Active dry yeast
2 T	Rosemary, fresh
¾ c	Water, warmed to 110°F
	Butter or shortening, for greasing bowl
2 T	Finely grated Parmesan cheese
2 T	Finely grated Romano cheese

Roast garlic: Preheat oven to 400°F. Turn a 6-inch wide piece of aluminum foil shiny side up. Place the garlic cloves in the middle. Carefully pour 2 tablespoons of olive oil over it. Wrap up the foil, so no oil escapes. Place foil packet in the oven on a rack and bake for 30 minutes.

Mix dry ingredients: In a medium bowl, mix flour, salt, sugar, black pepper, and yeast until blended.

Make dough: Dice the roasted garlic and add it to the dry ingredients. Chop the rosemary and add it. Add the remaining 2 tablespoons of olive oil and the warm water. Mix with a fork until a scraggly dough forms.

Knead dough: Turn dough out onto a floured work surface. Knead dough until it is smoothed out, about 30–40 turns. Grease the inside of a large bowl and place dough inside. Cover bowl with a clean dish towel. Allow dough to rise for 30 minutes. Punch the dough down and let it rise another 30 minutes.

Bake the bread: Increase oven temperature to 450°F. Cover a cookie sheet with parchment paper. Place dough in the center. Using your hands, shape dough into a flat circle, about 9 inches in diameter and 1½-inches thick. Brush top with olive oil. Sprinkle cheeses evenly across the top. Bake for 15–18 minutes. Remove from oven and let cool for 5 minutes. Cut and serve.

Makes 1 (9-inch) loaf.

Soups, Sauces

& Butters

CHILI

Chili has one purpose in the Gilmore food-o-sphere : Chili Fries. (Well, if you count Lorelai's request for chili-topped Pringles®, then make that two purposes.) Therefore, this chili isn't filled with chunks of tomato or a bunch of beans. No way. It's specifically designed to optimally complement french fries (or Pringles). Heap a big scoop of this stuff onto a big pile of fries, top it with grated cheese, and wash it down with a nice, hot cup of coffee, in true Gilmore fashion.

1 lb	80% lean ground beef
1	Yellow onion, finely chopped
3	Garlic cloves, smashed
1 T	Chili powder
1 t	Ground cumin
½ t	Dried oregano
½ t	Ground cinnamon
½ t	Kosher salt
¼ t	Ground black pepper
⅛ t	Cayenne
½ c	Tomato sauce
8 oz	Water
	Sour cream, optional for garnish
	Grated cheddar cheese, optional for garnish

Brown beef and onion: In a deep frying pan or a Dutch oven, add beef and chopped onion. Fry over medium-high heat, stirring often, until beef is mostly browned, a few pieces still showing a little pink. Add garlic and cook for an additional minute.

Spice and simmer: Add chili powder, cumin, oregano, cinnamon, salt, pepper, and cayenne to meat mixture. Then add tomato sauce and water. Stir until tomato sauce and water are fully combined, and the spices are evenly distributed.

Cook chili: Bring to a boil. Maintain a low boil for 10 minutes, stirring once a minute or so. Reduce heat to the lowest setting, and simmer for 20 minutes.

Serve: Remove garlic pieces from the chili and discard them. Spoon the chili into bowls (or on top of fries or your favorite canned potato chips) and garnish with a dollop of sour cream and/or grated cheddar cheese.

Makes 2–3 servings.

CHICKEN NOODLE SOUP

After years of bombarding her immune system with gallons of coffee and movie night trays full of junk food, Lorelai caught a cold. Not the sneeze-to-fake-you're-sick-so-the-old-people-will-leave-the-table-they've-been-hogging-for-an-hour sick, but a true cold. Of course she found her home remedy at Luke's: Chicken Noodle Soup with a side of Mashed Potatoes (see page 173), for breakfast, three days in a row.

She may not have been far off—homemade chicken soup has been touted as the home remedy for the common cold for many years. So the next time you feel that little tickle in the back of your throat, pass this recipe to a friend or loved one, pop your bottom lip out, and make your best Lorelai face. You'll be picking out the carrots in no time!

4	Celery stalks, tops and ends removed, chopped
3	Carrots, peeled, chopped
1	Yellow onion, peeled, chopped
1–2	Serrano peppers, stems removed, finely chopped
4 lbs	Chicken, whole or bone-in pieces
4 c	Homemade Chicken Broth (see page 93), or low-sodium packaged broth
	Water
1 T	Black pepper, ground
1 t	Kosher salt, or more to taste
1 t	Dried thyme
½ lb	Dried egg noodles
½ c	Minced fresh parsley

Boil the chicken: Using a Dutch oven, add the celery, carrots, onion, and serrano peppers to the bottom of the pan. Place the chicken/chicken pieces in next. Add the chicken broth. Add enough water to just cover chicken. Bring to a boil, over medium-high heat. Reduce heat to medium. Continue cooking at a low boil, without stirring, for 90 minutes.

Shred chicken: Using a straining spoon or two large forks, remove chicken/chicken pieces from the soup. Place them in a large bowl, to catch the liquids. Remove the meat from the chicken, and shred or chop it. Put 1½–2 cups of the chicken meat back into the soup. The remaining chicken may be stored and used for other recipes.

Make and serve the soup: Add black pepper, salt, thyme, and egg noodles to the soup. Simmer for 15 minutes or until noodles are tender. Stir in parsley until it is evenly blended into the soup. Serve.

Makes 6–8 servings.

HOMEMADE CHICKEN BROTH

SOOKIE'S KITCHEN

While this broth isn't strictly inspired by the show, it is needed for a lot of recipes. It's credited to Sookie because I figure she'd insist on using her own broth under any and all circumstances. She probably has quart after quart of the stuff neatly stored in the "chicken broth section" of her freezer, ready to use on the rare occasion when she doesn't have time to make it fresh.

If you have the time, it's definitely worth it to make this broth instead of using store-bought. It will add depth and dimension to the flavor of your dish, plus it comes with added health benefits. Make a batch as you need it, or make a double or triple batch to freeze for future use.

Recipes in this cookbook that use chicken broth include: Chicken Noodle Soup (page 91), Mock Turtle Soup (page 98), Open-Face Hot Turkey Sandwich (page 125), Risotto (page 141), Paella (page 153), Pancetta Chestnut Stuffing (page 175), and Lamb & Artichoke Stew (page 189).

1	Yellow onion, peeled, coarsely chopped
2	Garlic cloves, peeled, smashed
3	Carrots, peeled, coarsely chopped
4	Celery stalks, ends removed, coarsely chopped
1	Parsnip, peeled, coarsely chopped
1	Serrano pepper, stem removed, coarsely chopped
1	Whole chicken (3–4 lbs), giblets removed
12 c	Water
2	Fresh thyme sprigs
4	Fresh parsley sprigs
1 T	Black peppercorns
2 t	Kosher salt

Boil chicken: Add onion, garlic, carrots, celery, parsnip, serrano pepper, chicken, and water to a large pot or Dutch oven. Water should just cover the chicken and vegetables. Adjust as necessary. Over medium-high heat, bring to a boil. Reduce heat slightly. Cook at a low boil/simmer for 60 minutes.

Remove skin and meat from chicken: Carefully remove the chicken from the pot. Using two forks or a knife and a fork, remove the meat from the carcass. (The meat can be used for other dishes/recipes, but is no longer needed for this one.) Once the carcass is clean, return it to the water in the Dutch oven.

Make the broth: In addition to the carcass, add the thyme, parsley, peppercorns, and salt to the water. Bring the water to a boil again, then reduce heat and simmer for 60 minutes. Remove the carcass and discard. Strain the broth. If bits of herb or vegetable remain, strain twice. The resulting liquid is your broth!

Makes 6 cups.

MUSHROOM SOUP

CONTRIBUTED BY BARBIE SAYLOR KURT

The tasting session Sookie prepared for Emily's DAR event at the Independence Inn is the point where many of us learned the proper way to "taste" food. Prior to that episode, most of us would probably have taken one bite, then moved on. By watching the slow, thoughtful, deliberate paces Emily moved through, we learned the *proper* procedure. Taking three bites is the key: the first is to acclimate the pallet, the second is to serve as foundation, and the third bite is the time to judge.

You can use this soup to practice, or just go with Sookie's recommendation and serve this soup at your next important function. Between the soup and the string quartet, even your pickiest guests will be impressed.

32 oz	Vegetable broth
12 T	Unsalted butter
1	Shallot, very finely minced
18 oz	De-stemmed, sliced cremini mushrooms
9 oz	De-stemmed, sliced shiitake mushrooms
⅓ c	Flour
1 c	White wine
2 T	Chopped thyme leaves
1½ t	Kosher salt
1 t	Freshly ground black pepper
2 c	Half-and-half
2 T	Chopped Italian parsley, for garnish

Heat vegetable broth: In a large saucepan, heat vegetable broth to a slow simmer over medium heat.

Sauté shallot and mushrooms: In another large stockpot or cast enamel Dutch oven, melt the butter over medium-low heat. Then add the minced shallot, stir and cook until translucent. Add all of the mushrooms and cook for 15 minutes until softened, but not overdone.

Make the roux and deglaze pot: Add the flour, and cook for 2 minutes, stirring through. Be sure there is no raw flour remaining in the pot. Add the wine and cook for two more minutes, allowing the alcohol to cook off slightly, and stir, naturally deglazing the pot.

Make the soup: Add the vegetable broth, thyme leaves, salt, and pepper. Bring to a boil. Lower heat and simmer for 20 minutes. Add the half-and-half and heat through, but be careful not to boil.

Serve: Serve hot. Ladle into bowls or soup mugs. Top with a pinch of chopped parsley.

Makes 4–6 servings.

Note: *Regarding wine choices, I like to use an oaked chardonnay for an earthier flavor.*

ZUCCHINI SOUP

SOOKIE'S KITCHEN

Had Lorelai, Sookie, and Michel been asked to sleep in a zucchini patch all night during their tenure at the Independence Inn, they probably would have scoffed. But after they'd been faced with the many obstacles of opening the Dragonfly Inn—the fear of running out of money, the embarrassment of not paying the contractor, the annoyance of hiring a designer with a connection to Emily, the Canadian stove fiasco—suddenly sleeping in a zucchini patch seemed like the most natural thing to do. After all, Zucchini Soup was the only choice for opening night—they had to protect Jackson's crop.

It's no wonder they demanded this soup! It tastes fresh and healthy, yet also formal and a bit decadent. It's the absolute perfect choice for a grand opening.

	Olive oil
6	Zucchini, ends removed, chopped
2	White potatoes, peeled, chopped
1	Yellow onion, peeled, chopped
1	Serrano pepper, stem removed, chopped
4 c	Vegetable broth
½ c	Basil, fresh, chopped, packed
3 t	Kosher salt
1 T	Thyme, fresh
1 t	White pepper
½ t	Oregano, dried
¾ c	White wine, preferably chardonnay
½ c	Heavy whipping cream
½ c	Grated Parmesan cheese
2 t	Minced Italian parsley, fresh

Sauté vegetables: Using a Dutch oven, heat olive oil over medium-high heat for 2 minutes. Add zucchini, potatoes, onion, and serrano pepper. Turn the vegetables every 15–20 seconds so they cook evenly on all sides. Cook for roughly 5 minutes.

Boil vegetables: Add vegetable broth, basil, salt, thyme, white pepper, and oregano. Stir until spices are fully incorporated. Bring to a boil. Cook at a gentle boil for 12–15 minutes. When the potato pieces are soft, remove the pan from heat.

Blend soup: In batches, using a blender or food processor, blend soup until the chunks of vegetables turn into a smooth liquid. (Be careful not to burn yourself in the process.) Once all of the soup has been blended, return it to the stove.

Cook soup: Stir in the white wine, heavy cream, and Parmesan cheese. Simmer the soup over low heat for 10 minutes.

Serve soup: Ladle soup into bowls. Sprinkle with ¼ teaspoon minced parsley. Serve.

Makes 6–8 servings.

MOCK TURTLE SOUP

SOOKIE'S KITCHEN

Turtle soup was once a favorite of the upper echelon. However, once laws were put in place to protect turtles from being killed for their meat, other meats were substituted and the "mock" was added to the name. It's no wonder Richard remembered this soup from his childhood. When he was young, Mock Turtle Soup was very popular in both the UK and the US. Even major soup companies sold can after can of the stuff. Though its popularity has waned, this soup is still served in certain regions.

Now you can make your own at home! Once you do, chances are you'll understand why it was so special to him. With its combination of meats (each one chosen to mimic the different meat flavors and textures found in a turtle), this is one unique, tasty soup.

5	Roma tomatoes
	Water
4	Eggs
1 lb	Boneless, skinless chicken thighs
1 t	Salt
4 T	Butter, divided
1	Yellow onion, diced
3	Celery stalks, ends removed, finely chopped
2	Serrano peppers, stems removed, minced
1 lb	Beef loin, trimmed, cubed
2 c	Homemade Chicken Broth (see page 93), or low-sodium packaged broth
1 c	Cooking sherry
2 T	Flour
3	Garlic cloves, peeled, smashed
½ c	Chopped, fresh Italian parsley
6	Fresh Italian parsley sprigs, optional garnish

Puree tomatoes: Cut an "X" into the non-stem end of each tomato. In a medium saucepan, add tomatoes and ½ cup water. Bring to a boil over high heat. Boil for 1 minute. Move tomatoes to a colander and rinse with cold water for 20–30 seconds to blanch. This will loosen the tomato skins. Remove skins and discard. Put skinned tomatoes into blender and puree. Set aside.

Boil eggs: Gently place eggs in small saucepan and add just enough water to cover them. Cook over high heat until water begins to boil. Allow to boil for 8 minutes. Remove from heat. Let the eggs sit in the hot water for an additional 2 minutes. Then drain the hot water and replace with cold water. Let eggs sit for 1 minute. Remove eggs from water. Set aside.

Boil chicken: Add chicken thighs to a medium saucepan. Add just enough water to cover chicken. Add 1 teaspoon salt. Bring to a boil over medium-high heat. Reduce heat. Cook chicken at a gentle boil for about 15 minutes. Test a thigh at about 12 minutes by removing it from the water and cutting it in the middle. Look for pink in the middle. If you see pink, continue cooking for a few minutes. If no pink, chicken is done. Remove the thighs from the water and place them on a cutting board. Allow to cool for a few minutes. Then chop into ½-inch pieces. Set aside.

Brown beef and vegetables: In Dutch oven, melt 2 tablespoons butter over medium-high heat. Add onion, celery, serrano peppers, and beef. Stir every 20–30 seconds, until beef is browned and onion is translucent. Maintain the medium-high heat. Add chicken broth and sherry. Stir until fully combined.

Make roux: In small saucepan, melt the remaining 2 tablespoons butter over medium heat. Stir in flour with a fork to combine until a paste forms. Scrape the paste into the liquids in the Dutch oven. Stir continuously with a spatula or wooden spoon until the roux dissolves completely into the liquids. Continue stirring every 10–15 seconds. When liquids start to thicken, move on to the next step.

Make soup: Add chicken, tomato, garlic, and chopped parsley. Simmer over low heat for 20 minutes. Chop 2 eggs and add to soup. Simmer for 5 minutes. Remove from heat.

Serve soup: Remove garlic and discard. Ladle soup into bowls. Cut remaining 2 eggs into quarters, lengthwise. Garnish each bowl of soup with 1 egg quarter and a sprig of fresh parsley. Serve.

Makes 4–6 servings.

POTAGE AU CRESSON
(WATERCRESS SOUP)

Often throughout the seasons, Emily and Richard both show us how "international" they are by speaking beautiful French and even some Italian. Considering they visit Europe regularly, it makes sense they'd pick up new languages and customs. Emily likely got the idea for this soup on one of her trips abroad. Good thing she did—this soup is easy to make, healthy to the extreme, and the flavor impresses everyone, even ten-year-old girls.

2 T	Butter
1	Large shallot, peeled, thinly sliced
2 c	Watercress stems
1	Russet potato, peeled, diced
2 T	Thyme, fresh
1 t	Kosher salt
½ t	Ground black pepper
3 c	Water, divided
	Crème fraîche, for garnish, optional
	Chopped watercress leaves, for garnish, optional

Cook vegetables: In a Dutch oven, melt butter. Add shallot and sauté until lightly golden. Add watercress stems. Cook for 2 minutes, gently stirring once or twice. Add potato, thyme, salt, pepper, and 2 cups water. Boil for 12–15 minutes, until potato pieces are soft. Remove from heat.

Blend soup: Working in batches, blend soup in a blender or food processor until the chunks of vegetables turn into a smooth liquid. Return soup to Dutch oven.

Cook soup: Cook over medium-high heat. Add remaining 1 cup water and stir until soup is fully blended. Simmer for 10 minutes.

Serve Soup: Ladle soup into single-serving bowls. Garnish with a dollop of crème fraîche and a sprinkle of chopped watercress leaves. Serve.

Makes 2–3 servings.

PEACH SAUCE

This sauce tastes like the days between summer and fall, when kids are back to school, the days are still warm, mornings and evenings are crisp, and leaves are beginning to turn color. This sauce made its appearance in the show's pilot episode—which aired at the exact right time of year.

With their precise description, placement, and timing, "Peach Sauce" marked the first time the writers showed us "we're serious about this food stuff."

Try it for yourself, over waffles or pancakes or on a spoon; let it transport you back to those very early days in Stars Hollow.

4 c	Sliced, fresh peaches
1 T	Whole allspice
1 T	Whole cloves
1	Whole nutmeg
2 c	Water
3 T	Butter
3 T	Grand Marnier liqueur
3 T	Lemon juice, freshly squeezed
3 T	Maple syrup
1 T	Water
¼ c	Heavy cream, cold
2 T	Cornstarch

Boil and spice peaches: Add peach slices to a large saucepan. Tie allspice, cloves, and nutmeg in a spice bag and add to peaches. Add 2 cups water. Bring to a boil over medium-high heat. Continue to boil rapidly for 10 minutes, or until peaches become extremely soft. Remove spice bag.

Puree peaches: Pour the peach slices and their water into a blender. Blend until the mixture is fully pureed and there are no more solid peach pieces. Set aside.

Make Peach Sauce: In large saucepan, melt butter over medium heat. Add Grand Marnier, lemon juice, maple syrup, and 1 tablespoon water. Stir until fully combined. Strain peach puree into saucepan, discarding the pulp. Stir and heat until nearly boiling.

Thicken sauce, strain, and serve: Pour ¼ cup heavy cream into a measuring cup. Add 2 tablespoons cornstarch and stir. The mixture will become very thick—like sour cream. Add the mixture to the peach sauce; stir it in until it is fully dissolved. The peach sauce will become very thick with small lumps. Strain peach sauce one time to thin it a bit and remove lumps. Serve.

Makes 1½ cups.

4 TYPES OF PESTO

SOOKIE'S KITCHEN

If anyone can inspire a person to overachieve in the kitchen, it's Sookie. For a two-person picnic, she made all of these pestos, the Pineapple Cranberry Chutney (found on the next page), a selection of desserts, and a pretzel basket in which to carry it all. The first time we hear her mention four different pestos, it sounds like a lot of work. Turns out, of all the things she packed into that basket, the pestos are the quickest and easiest to make! Simply combine the ingredients, pour each one into a cute jar, tie a bit of ribbon, and you'll be on your way to raising top dollar at the auction.

Traditional Italian Pesto:

Herb or Vegetable:	1 c	Fresh basil leaves
Allium:	2	Garlic cloves, peeled
Nut or Seed:	2 T	Pine nuts
Cheese:	4 T	Parmesan
Oil:	⅓ c	Olive oil

Cilantro Pesto:

Herb or Vegetable:	1 c	Fresh cilantro leaves
Allium:	¼ c	Chopped red onion
Nut or Seed:	2 T	Slivered almonds
Cheese:	3 T	Cotija (or Asiago)
Additional Ingredient:	1 t	Crushed red pepper
Oil:	⅓ c	Avocado oil

Spicy Sun-dried Tomato Pesto:

Herb or Vegetable:	1 c	Sun-dried tomatoes, fresh or stored in olive oil
Allium:	2 T	Quartered, peeled shallots,
Nut or Seed:	2 T	Pecans
Cheese:	2 T	Asiago
Additional Ingredient:	1	Habanero, stem removed
Oil:	⅓ c	Olive oil

Sweet Mint Pesto:

Herb or Vegetable:	1 c	Fresh mint leaves
Allium:	8	Green onion whites, green parts removed
Nut or Seed:	2 T	Sunflower seeds
Cheese:	2 T	Feta
Additional Ingredient:	1 T	Honey
Oil:	⅓ c	Olive oil

Choose which pesto you'd like to make:

Add the herb/vegetable, allium, nut/seed, cheese, and additional ingredient (if there is one) for the desired pesto to a food processor or blender. Chop until the mixture becomes gritty—almost the consistency of a paste. Add oil. Chop again, until pesto forms. Remove from food processor/blender.

Serve.

Makes about ½ cup each.

PINEAPPLE CRANBERRY CHUTNEY

Here's another of Sookie's picnic creations. Even if bidding on a basket is not really your thing, keep in mind this chutney also can be paired with meat and fish, stirred into soups, and slathered on sandwiches.

Still, its combination of sweet and savory flavors must have tasted terrific with some soft cheese and crackers. Try it on your next picnic — whether it's outdoors or in your living room. You won't even miss the crinkle-cut carrot sticks.

2 T	Olive oil
2 c	Fresh pineapple
3 c	Cranberries, fresh or frozen
1 c	Diced red onion
1	Habanero pepper, stem removed, finely minced
½ c	Granulated sugar
1 t	Curry powder
⅓ c	Brandy

Cook fruit, onion, and pepper: Heat olive oil in a deep frying pan or Dutch oven over medium-high heat for 2 minutes. Add pineapple, cranberries, onion, and pepper. Stir to coat with oil. Cook, stirring often, until a reddish liquid forms on the bottom of the pan, about 12–15 minutes. Reduce heat.

Spice and simmer: Sprinkle mixture with sugar and curry. Add brandy. Stir to blend. Cover and simmer for 30 minutes, stirring occasionally. Remove from heat and serve.

Makes about 6 cups.

Note: *Habanero pepper provides the best flavor for this recipe. However, habanero peppers are very strong and can have adverse effects. If you'd prefer not to use habanero, substitute 2 serrano peppers.*

BUTTER

EMILY'S HOUSE

This recipe is being credited to Emily's House because only Emily could blame all the problems in her marriage on butter. Emily weathered Richard's untimely retirement, his health scares, his mother's visits, the oil stains on the driveway, his moustache, and the airing of his Pennilyn Lott secrets. But his failure to ask if she wanted butter—that was the ultimate insult, an oversight that relocated him to the pool house.

Butter is easy to make at home. Once you've tasted homemade butter on a muffin, roll, or scone, you'll want to experience its smooth, rich texture again and again. Just remember to offer some to the folks around you—you've seen what happens when you don't.

| 16 oz | Heavy whipping cream |
| ½ t | Kosher salt, or to taste |

Churn cream: Pour cream into a large mixing bowl. Using a mixer, mix cream on medium-low speed for 15–20 minutes. Increase speed as needed to keep up with the consistency of the cream.

Separate cream into butter and buttermilk: While mixing, the texture of the cream will change—from a shiny, smooth whipped cream, to a clotted, whipped cream, to a chunky, curdled consistency. Next, the fats will begin to separate from the liquids. A white, milky liquid will form at the bottom of the bowl. This is when the butter is about to form. Continue mixing until you have a ball of fats (butter) and a bowl of milk (buttermilk).

Remove buttermilk: Strain the buttermilk from the bowl. This may be saved for drinking or using in other recipes. With only the butter remaining in the bowl, mix again for 30 seconds. Drain any additional buttermilk.

Salt butter and serve: Add salt. Mix a final time for 30 seconds to blend the salt into the butter. Scrape the butter from the bowl and serve or store.

CINNAMON BUTTER

Gilmore Girls teaches us: when you want to crank up the autumn feels, spread some Cinnamon Butter on whatever you're eating. Whether it's Luke's Pumpkin Pancakes (page 45) or Sookie's Orange-Glazed Muffins (page 69), add a little Cinnamon Butter to make the air around you smell like fall.

1	**Batch of Butter (see page 109), minus salt**
1 c	**Water**
5	**Cinnamon sticks**
2 T	**Granulated sugar**
1 T	**Maple syrup**

Make butter: Mix the butter from page 109, but do not add salt.

Make cinnamon water: In a small saucepan, add water and cinnamon sticks. Bring to boil over medium-high heat. Continue to boil until water has reduced by two-thirds. Discard cinnamon sticks. Add sugar and maple syrup. Stir until both fully dissolve. Remove from heat and allow to cool until liquid is room temperature.

Make cinnamon butter: Using a mixer, mix cinnamon liquid into butter until fully blended. Remove butter from bowl. Serve or store.

Burgers & Sandwiches

CHEESEBURGER

All hail Luke's Cheeseburger—the Grand Poobah of the Gilmore girls' diet! It holds so much power in their lives, it should wear a big red hat! (If you flip to the next page, it does!)

After seeing this burger on the screen, episode after episode—every lunch, every dinner, the post–golf outing, the post–coming out party, the "rant meal," the "acceptance meal"—it's possibly the one Gilmore food fans would most like to try in real life.

So here's your chance—serve yourself a Cheeseburger from Luke's! Just remember to hold your pinkie finger out when you eat it.

2	Sesame seed buns
1 lb	Lean beef, ground
1 t	Kosher salt, divided
1 t	Black pepper, divided
2	Cheddar cheese slices, optional
	Grilled onions, optional
	Sautéed mushrooms, optional

Optional Garnish:

1	Red onion, sliced thinly
1	Tomato, sliced
4	Lettuce leaves
12	Pickle chips

Prepare buns and garnish: On two separate plates, arrange a sesame seed bun, open, on each. Beside each bun, arrange garnish. Set aside.

Make hamburger patties: Divide the ground beef in half. Roll each half into a ball; then, between your palms, flatten it to ¾-inch thickness. Place the flattened patties onto a plate. Season each patty with ½ teaspoon of kosher salt and ½ teaspoon of black pepper.

Fry patties: Heat a large skillet over medium-high heat for 1 minute. Place the hamburger patties onto the skillet, leaving space between them. (Cook patties one at a time if both won't fit in your skillet at once.) After 3 minutes, flip the patties. Cook for an additional 2 minutes. Remove from heat. Add a cheese slice to each patty, if desired. Let patties sit in skillet for an additional 2 minutes. Place each patty on a bun and serve.

Makes 2 cheeseburgers.

Grilled Onions: Thinly slice 1 yellow onion. Separate each slice into rings. Melt 4 tablespoons butter in frying pan. Add onions. Use spatula to flip onions a few times to coat them evenly with butter. Season with ¼ teaspoon each: salt, black pepper, smoked paprika, and granulated garlic. Continue flipping every 20–30 seconds for 5 minutes or until onions become tender and golden brown. Serve.

Sautéed Mushrooms: Heat 2 tablespoons olive oil or butter in large frying pan. Add 3 cups sliced white mushrooms. Use spatula to flip mushrooms a few times to coat them evenly with oil/butter. Season with ¼ teaspoon each: salt, black pepper, smoked paprika, and granulated garlic. Continue flipping every 20–30 seconds for 5 minutes or until mushrooms become tender. Serve.

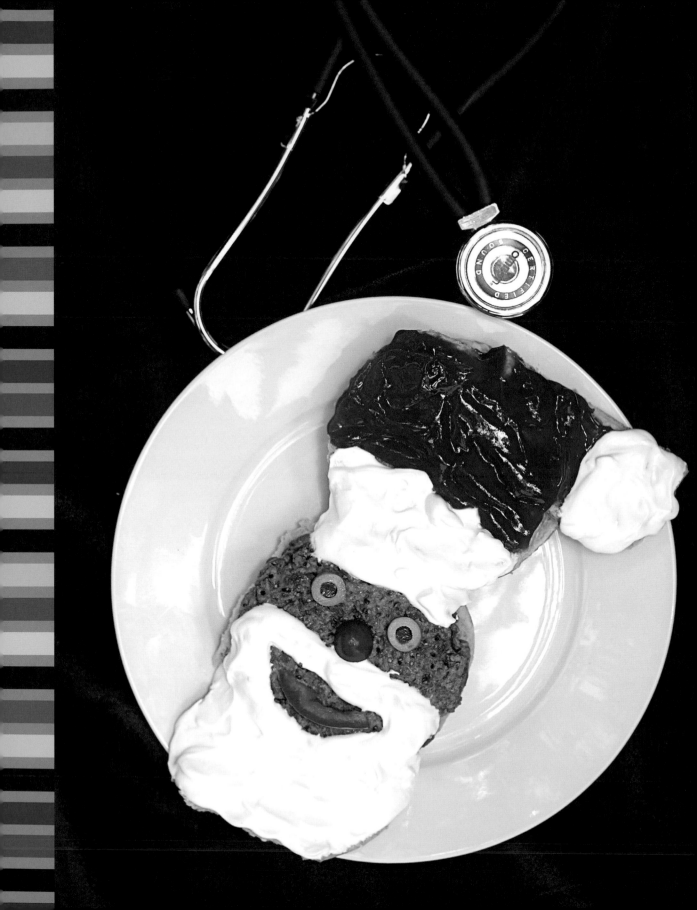

SANTA BURGER

Luke made this for Lorelai on Christmas Eve—the year she was uninvited from celebrating Christmas at her parents' house. After Rory left for Hartford, alone and dejected, Lorelai wandered into Luke's Diner for some company. To boost her spirits, Luke made this burger. Even though Lorelai called it disgusting, her body language revealed how much she liked that he made it for her. She didn't eat it, though. It's recommended you don't either. The Santa Burger is a gesture, not a meal.

2	**Large hamburger buns**
1	**Cooked hamburger patty (see page 115)**
½ c	**Sour cream, cold**
½ c	**Ketchup, cold**
2	**Small green olives, stuffed with pimento**
1	**Cherry tomato**
1	**Roma tomato**

Prep and arrange buns:

1. Separate 2 buns. Cut 1 top bun in half and move one half down for Santa's beard . . .

2. Stack top & bottom of Bun 2; square off bottom for Santa's hat . . .

3. Cut off corner of hat . . .

4. Move last bun half in position for pom.

Position burger: Pat hamburger patty on both sides with a paper towel to soak up some of the grease. Place it atop the center bun.

Fill in sour cream: Fill a pastry bag or squirt bottle with the sour cream. Use it to draw a "moustache" in a straight line across the bottom third of the patty. Then outline that bottom third of the patty with a half circle of sour cream. Fill in everything below that line with sour cream—including the half of Bun 1—to form the "beard."

About ½ inch from the top of the patty, using the sour cream, draw a straight line across the patty. Create a rectangle of sour cream, about 2 inches tall. This is the "white fur trim" of Santa's hat. Fill in the "cotton ball" pom of Santa's hat by placing a circle of sour cream, about 1 inch in diameter, on the very outer tip of Santa's hat.

Fill in ketchup: Fill a pastry bag or squirt bottle with ketchup. Fill in everything between the "cotton ball" and the "white fur trim" with ketchup to make "Santa's hat."

Add face: Cut the top and bottom off each olive, leaving 2 "eyes." Position these on the patty just below the "white fur trim." Cut the cherry tomato in half. Place one half, cut-side down, in the center of the patty, right above the "moustache" (discard the other half). Cut a ¼-inch center slice of the Roma tomato. Cut the slice in half, discard seeds, leaving two "smiles"—position one of them between the "mustache" and "beard." Discard the other. Voilà!

Makes 1 Santa Burger.

TURKEY BURGER

LUKE'S DINER

Known for introducing his cheeseburger by saying "dead cow" and for blathering on about the negative effects of eating red meat, Luke leaves fans asking, "If he's so anti-red meat why does he serve it all day long to his customers?" No one knows. It's just one of the little character nuances fans love about the townspeople of Stars Hollow.

What we do see is, in the privacy of his own apartment, he makes and eats Turkey Burgers. You can, too—they offer all the same fun of a burger, with none of the judgment.

4	Wheat buns
2 T	Olive oil, divided
1	Yellow onion, medium, grated
3	Garlic cloves, large, minced
1 lb	Ground turkey
1 t	Worcestershire sauce
1 t	Crushed red pepper
1 t	Kosher salt, divided
1 t	Black pepper, divided
4	Muenster cheese slices, optional

Optional Garnish:

1	Red onion, sliced thinly
1	Tomato, sliced
4	Lettuce leaves
12	Pickle chips

Prepare buns and garnish: On 4 separate plates, arrange a wheat bun, open, on each. Beside each bun, arrange garnish. Set aside.

Cook onion and garlic: In a large skillet, heat 1 tablespoon olive oil over medium-high heat for about a minute. Distribute evenly the grated onion and minced garlic around the skillet. Using a spatula, every 15 seconds or so, move the mixture around the skillet so it cooks evenly on all sides. Once the water from the onion has evaporated and the edges of the garlic begin to turn golden brown, remove from heat. Set aside and let cool for 5 minutes.

Season meat: In a large mixing bowl, combine ground turkey, Worcestershire sauce, and crushed red pepper. Add onions-and-garlic mixture. Evenly work all ingredients into the meat, using your hands.

Make turkey burger patties: Once all ingredients are combined, divide the mixture into 4 sections. Roll each section into a ball; then, between your palms, flatten it to ¾-inch thickness. Place each flattened patty onto a plate. Season each patty with ¼ teaspoon of kosher salt and ¼ teaspoon of black pepper.

Fry patties: Using the same large skillet, heat the remaining tablespoon of olive oil over medium-high heat for 1 minute. Place the turkey patties into the skillet, leaving space between them. (Cook patties two at a time, if all 4 won't fit in your skillet at once.) After four minutes, flip the patties. Cook for an additional 3 minutes. Remove from heat. Add a cheese slice to each patty, if desired. Let patties sit in skillet for an additional 2 minutes. Place each patty on a wheat bun and serve.

Makes 4 burgers.

MONTE CRISTO SANDWICH

Lorelai said this sandwich sounds like deep-fried soup. She's obviously never had one. The Monte Cristo is a classic. It's as close as one can get to eating a sandwich wrapped in a donut, without actually eating a sandwich wrapped in a donut. The savory of the meats balances perfectly with the sweetness of the confectioners' sugar and red currant jam. The fried outer coating gives each bite a satisfying crunch. Lorelai is missing out—this is one of the very best sandwiches, ever. Even April knows that!

1	Egg
¾ c	Water
¼ c	Half-and-half
1 c	Flour
1 t	Baking powder
	Vegetable oil
4	Egg bread slices (or white bread)
2 T	Mustard
2 T	Mayonnaise
4	Deli ham slices
4	Deli turkey slices
4	Havarti cheese slices
½ c	Confectioners' sugar
½ c	Red currant jelly

Make batter: In a shallow bowl, whisk egg until it's blended. Add water and half-and-half. Whisk. Add flour and baking powder. Whisk until smooth.

Heat oil: Fill Dutch oven or very deep frying pan with vegetable oil until oil is about 2 inches deep. Place over medium-high heat. Insert a candy thermometer into oil and keep it there until oil reaches 360°F.

Assemble sandwiches: Set out all 4 pieces of bread. Spread mustard on 2 slices, mayonnaise on 2 slices. Place two ham slices on each mustard-covered slice. Place two turkey slices on each mayonnaise-covered slice. Place a piece of cheese on each of the four stacks. Flip each turkey side over and place it atop a ham side. You now have two sandwiches.

Batter and cook sandwiches: Dip one sandwich into the batter until it's fully coated on one side, then flip it to coat the other side. Ensure batter is covering the outside edge as well. Carefully place the battered sandwich into the hot oil using tongs and/or a spatula. Repeat for the second sandwich. Allow the sandwiches to cook on one side for 2–3 minutes, or until the side is dark, golden brown. Using tongs, flip and cook the other side of the sandwiches for 2 minutes. Once both sides are dark golden brown, remove the sandwiches from the oil and place them on wire racks. Allow sandwiches to cool for 2–3 minutes.

Cut, dust, and serve sandwiches: Place each sandwich on a cutting board. Using a large, sharp knife, cut the sandwich in the shape of an "X," to create 4 small triangles. Place 4 triangles on each plate, crust-side down. Dust with confectioners' sugar. Serve each with a side of red currant jelly.

Makes 2 sandwiches.

CHICKEN CHOW MEIN SANDWICH

This cookbook would not be a true reflection of Gilmore life without including a recipe calling for Chinese take-out, in order to make a dish from Al's Pancake World. The Chicken Chow Mein Sandwich may sound like a lot of unnecessary bread. It isn't.

Eating Chicken Chow Mein on a toasted roll is a mind-broadening experience. It'll make you question your life choices—like your love for Pop-Tarts, or your preference for wearing your hair down. It's that good.

2 T	Butter
4	Fresh French rolls, sliced down center
2 qts	Chicken chow mein, delivered from local Chinese restaurant
	Soy sauce, optional
4	Fortune cookies, for garnish

Order chow mein: Call or use a food-ordering app on your mobile phone to contact a local Chinese restaurant. Request 2 orders of chicken chow mein (or "pan-fried noodles," if that's how it's listed on their menu). Wait until it arrives.

Toast rolls: (Depending on the size of your skillet, toast 1 or 2 rolls at a time.) For each roll, melt ½ tablespoon of butter. Take care to distribute the butter evenly around the skillet. Once melted, place the roll(s) cut-side down in the butter. Scoot the roll(s) around the pan until all of the butter is absorbed. Toast the roll(s) for about a minute, until the toasted side is a nice golden color. Remove each roll to its own plate, toasted side up. Repeat until all 4 rolls are toasted.

Assemble sandwiches: Using tongs or two forks, scoop half of a container of chow mein onto each toasted roll. Make sure to get a good ratio of noodles to chicken on each sandwich. If desired, season each sandwich with soy sauce. Garnish with a fortune cookie. Serve.

Makes 4 sandwiches.

OPEN-FACE HOT TURKEY SANDWICH

Sometimes things we watch happen in Stars Hollow don't happen in real life. For instance, if the chef from a local inn walked into a diner to eat, then suddenly walked behind the counter and started garnishing people's orders, it would seem a little odd, if not alarming. When Sookie did this very thing in Luke's, she hardly got any reaction at all (except from Luke)! Is this one of the reasons fans of the show love life in the hollow so much? Because folks interact differently there — a little closer, a little more open, not so worried about "the rules"?

Something to contemplate as you tuck into this soul-soothing comfort food.

Mushroom Gravy:

2 T	Butter
2 T	Flour
2 c	Homemade Chicken Broth (see page 93), or low-sodium packaged broth
2 t	Lemon juice, freshly squeezed
¼ t	Cayenne pepper
	Sautéed mushrooms (page 115)

Turkey Sandwich:

2 T	Butter, room temperature
4	White bread slices
1 c	Mushroom gravy, from above or store-bought gravy
½ lb	Deli turkey, sliced
1 t	Chopped fresh thyme leaves, optional

Make gravy: Melt butter in medium saucepan over medium-high heat. Sprinkle in flour and stir with a fork until fully combined. Continue to heat, for about 30 seconds. Add chicken broth, lemon juice, and cayenne — whisk together until the flour-butter mixture (the roux) is fully blended into the liquid. Whisk/stir occasionally. After 4 or 5 minutes the liquid will begin to thicken. This is your gravy. Add in the mushrooms (liquids and all) and stir. Reduce heat to a low simmer.

Toast bread on one side: Heat a large frying pan over medium-high heat. Spread ½ tablespoon of butter evenly on one side of each slice of bread. Once pan is hot, place each slice of bread, butter side down, into pan. Cook for 2 minutes or until the bread is golden and toasted on one side. Remove the bread from pan—using two plates, place 2 slices of bread on each, toasted side down.

Heat the turkey: Pour 1 cup of the gravy into the frying pan. Then add turkey. Coat turkey with gravy as evenly as possible. Cook turkey for 90 seconds on each side. Using a spatula, remove turkey from the pan and place the slices on top of the bread—evenly distribute it between the 4 slices.

Top with gravy and serve: Ladle gravy onto each slice of bread. Sprinkle ½ teaspoon of fresh thyme leaves on each sandwich. Serve.

Makes 2 sandwiches.

PATTY MELT

The Patty Melt is one of Kirk's favorites. He eats every meal at Luke's—so if this is his favorite, it must be great! Of course there is no physical way Kirk could spend his days sitting in the diner, while holding down nearly every job in town, kowtowing to his mother's wishes, befriending multiple widows, producing a short film, and romancing Lulu. It's just not possible. Kirk is the townsperson for whom we suspend reality. It's fun.

So when he's suddenly in so much of a rush that he doesn't have time to wait for a Patty Melt, it makes no sense. Kirk has time for everything!

Don't be like Kirk—make time for the Patty Melt.

½ lb	Ground beef
½ t	Salt
½ t	Black pepper
2 T	Olive oil
4	Gouda slices
1 c	Grilled onions (page 115)
4	Rye bread slices
	Dill pickle spears, for garnish

Cook hamburger patties: Divide ground beef into two ¼-pound patties. Shape the patties, roughly, into the shape of the rye bread you are using. Season each patty with ⅛ teaspoon salt and ⅛ teaspoon black pepper on each side. Preheat a large frying pan over medium-high heat for 2 minutes. Add patties to pan. Cook for 3–4 minutes on each side. Remove patties from pan and place on paper towels to remove excess oils. Use extra paper towels to wipe the frying pan, removing most of the oils and charred pieces.

Cook sandwiches: Over medium-high heat, heat the olive oil in the same large fry pan for 2 minutes. Make sure the oil is evenly distributed, covering the entire bottom of the pan. Set the bread into the oil so each piece is lying flat, without any overlapping. Quickly place a cheese slice on each slice of bread. Set a cooked patty on top of two of these cheesy bread slices. Top each patty with a heaping ½ cup of grilled onions. Using a spatula, flip the remaining cheesy bread slices onto the top of each onion-topped patty. Once the bottom bread is a medium golden brown, carefully flip the sandwich and cook the other side to the same golden brown. Remove from pan. Place the sandwiches on cutting board and cut in half, diagonally. Plate the sandwiches. Garnish with dill pickle spears. Serve.

Makes 2 sandwiches.

GRILLED CHEESE

If you're in Luke's Diner during a rush, you'll catch multiple glimpses of Grilled Cheese sandwiches whizzing past. This is one popular sandwich—among children and adults, alike. Lane, being the superstar server she is, devised the perfect way to serve a Grilled Cheese. To prevent the pickle juice from meandering over to the sandwich and making the bread soggy, Lane places one french fry between the two—so the pickle juice stays on its side, and the bread stays crispy. Brilliant!

Who knew *Gilmore Girls* could be so educational?

2	White bread slices, quality
2	Muenster cheese slices
1	Cheddar cheese slice (use 2 if slices are thin)
1 T	Butter
1	Dill pickle spear, for garnish

Prep bread and cheese: Arrange bread slices side by side. Place a piece of Muenster cheese on each bread slice. Place the slice of cheddar on top one of the Muenster slices. Set aside.

Cook sandwich: In a medium skillet, over medium-high heat, melt the butter. Distribute it evenly across bottom of skillet. Once fully melted, place both halves of the sandwich, bread-side down, onto the skillet. Taking care to keep the cheese in place, with a spatula, scoot the bread around a little so each slice soaks up half of the butter. Once all of the butter has been absorbed, flip one cheese-topped bread slice onto the other. Fry the sandwich for roughly 90 seconds. Once the bottom bread has turned an even golden color, flip the sandwich. Cook the second side for another 90 seconds. Remove from heat. Let sandwich rest in skillet for another 30 seconds, to give the cheese additional time to melt.

Serve: Remove sandwich to a cutting board. Cut it in half, diagonally. Place on a plate. Serve with a dill pickle spear.

Makes 1 sandwich.

TUNA MELT

LUKE'S DINER

Every diner in America offers this sandwich, so when we hear Luke or Lane or Caesar call out "Tuna Melt!," it makes Luke's Diner seem a little more authentic. Perhaps that's why it was mentioned in the show now and then; to make the whole "diner experience" seem more real and to make us feel as though we were sitting right there at a table by the window, wondering if Luke coddled his eggs.

If you want to amp up that "just like being there" feeling even more, make one of these sandwiches for yourself at home and have it while you watch your favorite diner scenes. Since you're the proprietor, you won't even need to tip!

5 oz	Canned albacore tuna
1 T	Finely chopped celery
1 T	Finely chopped green onion, white part only
1 T	Finely chopped green onion, green part only
1 t	Lemon juice, freshly squeezed
3 t	Olive oil, divided
½ t	Black pepper
4	Sourdough bread slices
4	Cheese slices (Gouda recommended)
	Dill pickle spears, for garnish

Make tuna salad: In a small bowl, with a fork, combine tuna, celery, green onion (both parts), lemon juice, 1 teaspoon olive oil, and the black pepper. Continue to work the ingredients into the tuna until evenly combined.

Assemble sandwiches: Top one slice of bread with half of the tuna salad. Flatten the tuna salad with a fork, so it's evenly spread across the bread. Top the tuna salad with 2 slices of cheese, then another slice of bread. Repeat these steps with the other half of the tuna salad.

Fry sandwiches: Heat a large frying pan over medium-high heat for 2 minutes. Brush each side of both sandwiches with ½ teaspoon of olive oil. Place sandwiches in pan and cook for 2–3 minutes, until bottom side is a dark golden brown. Using a spatula, flip the sandwiches and cook for an additional 2 minutes. Remove from heat, but keep sandwiches in pan for 2–3 additional minutes. The sandwiches will slowly continue to cook. This will help the cheese to fully melt. Remove sandwiches from pan and place them on a cutting board. Using a large, sharp knife, cut each sandwich in half, diagonally. Plate each sandwich. Serve with a dill pickle spear.

Makes 2 sandwiches.

HIGH TEA: PEANUT BUTTER & JELLY SANDWICHES

Good for Sookie, thinking a group of ten-year-old girls at a high tea would prefer a kid-friendly finger sandwich made out of peanut butter and jelly. After blundering her way through that kids' birthday party a few years earlier, she certainly redeemed herself here, proving that motherhood taught her what kids like to eat.

Emily, in contrast, never learned and/or never cared. In her world, children eat the same sandwiches as adults, so they learn the proper etiquette of society.

Which philosophy suits you? If it's Sookie's, enjoy these fun, tasty little treats. If it's Emily's, see you on the next page.

8	Thinly cut (¼-inch thickness), fresh, white bread slices, high quality
2 T	Cinnamon butter (page 111)
¼ c	Creamy peanut butter
¼ c	Red currant jelly

Make sandwiches: Arrange bread slices side by side on work surface. Spread a thin layer of cinnamon butter on each slice. On 4 slices, spread the peanut butter, 1 tablespoon per slice. On the other 4 slices, spread the jelly, 1 tablespoon per slice. Place each peanut-buttered slice atop a jelly slice.

Cut and serve: Using a large, sharp knife, square off each sandwich by cutting the bread crust off each side. Cut each sandwich into 4 pieces—either triangles, rectangles, or squares. Arrange them on a serving platter. Serve.

Makes 16 tea sandwiches.

HIGH TEA: CUCUMBER MINT SANDWICHES

Rather wisely, Emily didn't want to serve the girls spinach because some of them wore braces. She instructed Sookie to make these instead.

Traditionally, cucumber sandwiches encountered at luncheons and high teas can be tasteless, bland, or just plain boring. Not these. The lemon juice and chile pepper turn them into a Sookie-esque creation by adding some tang and a tiny bit of heat.

Serve them at your next cotillion or British-themed going away party.

Minty Cream Cheese Spread:

4	Garlic cloves
1½ c	Fresh mint leaves
1 c	Fresh cilantro
½ c	Minced green onion
1	Green chile pepper/ Anaheim chile pepper
½ t	Salt
1 T	Lemon juice, freshly squeezed
8 oz	Cream cheese, room temperature
8	Thinly cut (¼-inch thickness), fresh, white bread slices, high quality
4 T	Butter, room temperature
2	Persian cucumbers, thinly sliced

Make Minty Cream Cheese Spread: Combine garlic, mint, cilantro, green onion, chile, salt, and lemon juice in a blender or food processor. Chop or stir until all ingredients are combined and form a paste-like consistency. Scrape the mixture into a medium mixing bowl. Add cream cheese. Using a fork, combine the two until fully blended.

Assemble sandwiches: Arrange bread slices flat on work surface. Spread a very light layer of butter on each slice. On 4 slices, spread a thick layer of the cream cheese spread, then cucumber slices in 2 layers. Place the 4 slices of remaining buttered bread atop each cucumber-topped slice of bread. Wrap each sandwich tightly in plastic wrap and refrigerate for 30 minutes.

Cut and serve: Remove plastic wrap from sandwiches. Place sandwiches on cutting board. Using a large, sharp knife, cut crusts off all four sides of each sandwich. Cut each sandwich into 4 pieces—either triangles, rectangles, or squares. Arrange them on a serving platter. Serve.

Makes 16 tea sandwiches.

HIGH TEA: SMOKED SALMON CREAM CHEESE SANDWICHES

SOOKIE'S KITCHEN

Though her Peanut Butter & Jelly Sandwiches were harshly dismissed as "circus food," Sookie redeemed herself by delighting hard-to-please Emily with these healthy little bites.

The flavors in this recipe combine to produce such delicious finger sandwiches, you may feel tempted to skip cutting them altogether, and just eat a whole sandwich yourself. Emily definitely would not approve, but who's telling?

Herbed Cream Cheese Spread:

8 oz	Cream cheese
¼ c	Finely chopped, fresh dill
¼ c	Finely chopped, fresh parsley
¼ c	Finely chopped, fresh chives
1 T	Lemon juice, freshly squeezed
½ t	Kosher salt
¼ t	Black pepper
8	Thinly cut (¼-inch thickness), fresh, dense whole grain bread slices, high quality
10 oz	Smoked salmon, sliced
½	Red onion, very thinly sliced

Make Herbed Cream Cheese Spread: In medium mixing bowl, using a fork, mix cream cheese, dill, parsley, chives, lemon juice, salt, and pepper until fully combined with a smooth consistency.

Assemble sandwiches: Arrange bread slices flat on work surface. On 4 slices, spread a thick layer of the cream cheese spread, then salmon slices. Top each with a thin layer of red onion slices. Place the remaining 4 slices on top of the salmon-and-onion-topped slices. Wrap each sandwich tightly in plastic wrap and refrigerate for 30 minutes.

Cut and serve: Remove plastic wrap from sandwiches. Place sandwiches on cutting board. Using a large, sharp knife, cut crusts off all four sides of each sandwich. Cut each sandwich into 4 pieces—either triangles, rectangles, or squares. Arrange them on a serving platter. Serve.

Makes 16 tea sandwiches.

Tester—Art Gonzales

Pasta & Rice Dishes

RISOTTO

SOOKIE'S KITCHEN

Risotto is one of the most iconic dishes from *Gilmore Girls*. Not only is it the dish Sookie made for her dying mother, thus extending her life for three years; it's also the dish she remade for the food critic, before stalking him at home with a covered dish of the stuff and a glass of white wine.

The process for making this dish takes some patience—but it's worth it. If you give yourself some time to leisurely stir the broth into the rice until its starches are released, you'll be rewarded with a creamy, rich, authentic Italian primo (first course). Will it extend your life? Probably not. But it will definitely add some magic to your meal.

1 c	Finely shredded Parmesan
½ c	Chopped, fresh basil
6 c	Homemade Chicken Broth (see page 93), or low-sodium packaged broth
30–40	Saffron strands
1½ c	Arborio rice
2 T	Butter
1	Shallot, peeled & minced
½ c	Dry white wine (chardonnay recommended)
1 t	Kosher salt

Prep cheese and basil: These will be needed in a hurry once the risotto is cooked.

Heat broth and rinse rice: In a large saucepan, heat the broth over medium heat. Once the broth is warm/hot, add the saffron strands and stir. Let the broth continue to warm on the stove for 15 minutes. Meanwhile, pour the rice into a bowl. Fill the bowl with water, then swish the rice around until the water turns milky white. Rinse the rice in a strainer. Pour the rice back into the bowl and repeat these steps four times, or until the water no longer turns white. Rinse the rice a final time, very well. Set aside.

Sauté shallot: On a burner (near the burner with the broth), in a Dutch oven, melt the butter over medium heat. Once melted, add the shallot. Sauté for 2–3 minutes, until the shallot turns translucent but before it begins to brown around the edges. Add the white wine. Stir.

Cook the rice: Add the rice to the white wine mixture. Stir it in, and continue stirring until the liquids have been absorbed. Stir 1 cup of the broth (about 2 ladles-full) and a generous pinch of salt into the rice. Continue stirring until liquids have been absorbed. Continue adding the broth, 1 cup at a time, and the salt, one pinch at a time, stirring the rice until the liquids are absorbed. Once 5 cups of broth have been added, taste the rice before adding more broth/salt. The rice should be soft to bite into, and the center should be very slightly firm (not hard). If the rice appears "done" after 5 cups of broth, there is no need to add more; if the rice is not quite "done," add a little more broth as needed. Once the rice is "done," proceed to the next step.

Make the Risotto: Stir the Parmesan and basil into the rice. Spoon the mixture into bowls. Top with additional cheese, if desired. Serve.

Makes 2 large or 4 small servings.

Testers—Bridget Kushiyama & Shawn Kushiyama

BEEF-A-RONI

EMILY'S HOUSE

Well, Rory brought her beautiful, unsuspecting boyfriend, Dean, to a special edition of Friday Night Dinner. At the table, going against all proper etiquette, Richard turned into Attack Grandpa, practically shining a light in Dean's face, while drilling him with questions. Chaos ensued. Dean was bewildered, Rory was furious, Emily tried to regain control of the evening, and Lorelai kept inserting Lorelai-isms in an attempt to distract her father. Even with all of this going on, still the most important part of this dinner was the food. Why? Because Emily had her staff make a version of Beefaroni®, of all things, from scratch.

Yes, sure—Emily let it drop that the secret to the recipe is that it's not "beef." (It's actually just a type of meat-free filler.) But don't worry about that. This version is beef and tastes so close to the original, your children (including adult children, and adults who were once children) may never know the difference.

1 lb	Ziti pasta (pasta al ceppo or mini penne will give similar effect)
1 t	Olive oil
1 lb	Ground beef, lean or extra lean
1½ t	Kosher salt
1 t	Sugar
¼ t	Black pepper
½ t	Granulated garlic
3¼ c	Chopped tomatoes
½ c	Grated cheddar cheese
15 oz	Tomato sauce
2 c	Water
3 T	Lemon juice, freshly squeezed

Cook pasta: Follow instructions on package to cook pasta until it is soft to bite into. Strain. Pour olive oil onto pasta and stir, to keep it from sticking together. Set aside.

Brown ground beef: Place ground beef into a Dutch oven. Brown the meat over medium-high heat. As it cooks, use a wooden spoon or spatula to break the meat down into small pieces. Once it is browned, sprinkle with salt, sugar, pepper, and granulated garlic. Stir to combine and cook for 1 minute. Using a slotted spoon, remove the beef from the pot and place it into a blender. Set aside.

Heat chopped tomatoes: Return the Dutch oven with the remaining grease to medium-high heat. Add the chopped tomatoes. Stir to combine. Once the mixture is hot, add grated cheese. Stir until cheese melts and dissolves.

Blend beef and tomatoes: Carefully spoon or pour tomato-cheese mixture into blender with beef. Turn on blender and continue to mix contents until beef is completely liquefied and combined with tomatoes. (Be careful as mixture will be hot!)

Make Beef-a-Roni: Pour contents of blender back into Dutch oven. Add tomato sauce, 2 cups water, and lemon juice. Stir until water is completely incorporated. Over medium-high heat, bring sauce to a low boil. Reduce heat and add pasta. Stir until combined. Simmer for 10 minutes. Spoon into bowls. Serve.

Makes 4–6 servings.

Tester—Amanda True

MAC & CHEESE

When you think of Mac & Cheese on *Gilmore Girls*, which character pops into your mind? Quite possibly, it's Paris. More than once, we saw her get excited, verging on giddy, at the thought of eating Mac & Cheese. The night Jess brought Rory a truckload of food from Luke's, Paris got to indulge, and boy was she happy. Afterward, she even acted like a true girlfriend by helping defend Rory from an angry, suspicious Dean.

This is a quick and easy dish to prepare. The Monterey Jack cheese in between the pasta layers adds that ooey gooey deliciousness—the hallmark of a great Mac & Cheese.

	Water
¼ t	Salt
1 lb	Dried pasta (cellentani-style cork screw pasta recommended)
2 c	Grated Monterey Jack cheese
10 T	Butter
½ c	Flour
3½ c	Whole milk
2 c	Cubed processed cheese (Velveeta® recommended)
2 c	Grated medium cheddar cheese

Prep oven: Place oven rack in the center position. Preheat oven to 350°F.

Cook pasta: In a Dutch oven or large saucepan, bring water to a boil over medium-high heat. Add salt then add pasta. Stir. Cook 5–6 minutes only. Pasta will still be hard in the center. Use a strainer to drain the water. Arrange half the pasta in a flat layer using a 10x15-inch baking pan. Evenly sprinkle half of the Monterey Jack cheese. Use the remaining pasta to add a second layer. Sprinkle the remaining Monterey Jack cheese evenly across the second layer. Set aside.

Make cheese sauce: In a large saucepan, melt butter over medium-high heat. Add flour and stir until the two are fully combined into a yellowish paste. Stir in milk. Continue stirring and heat for 5–7 minutes. Once the sauce begins to thicken, add processed cheese and cheddar cheese. Stir until cheese has melted.

Bake: Pour the sauce over the pasta/Monterey Jack layers, until all sections are covered. Bake for 15 minutes. Remove from oven and serve hot.

Makes 6–8 servings.

Tester—Sarah Lea Phelps

MACARONI & CHEESE
IN A JALAPEÑO-CHIPOTLE CREAM SAUCE

One of the most intriguing dishes to come from *Gilmore Girls* is this "adults only" Macaroni & Cheese. When Sookie pulled its green, baked gooiness from the oven and offered it to Lorelai as the "kids' food"—well, that was painful to watch. It was the tell-tale sign that all was not well in Preggoville. Though, thanks to Sookie's panic attack, we have this inspired dish.

	Butter or shortening, for preparing pan
8 c	Water
3 T	Olive oil, divided
3 t	Kosher salt, divided
1 lb	Farfalle (bow tie) pasta
3	Large jalapeño peppers, coarsely chopped
1	Garlic cloves, cut in two
2 T	Coarsely chopped chipotle peppers
4 T	Butter
4 T	Flour
4 c	Whole milk
1 c	Grated sharp white cheddar cheese

Prep oven and pan: Ensure oven rack is placed in the middle of oven. Preheat oven to 350°F. Grease a 9x13-inch baking pan.

Cook pasta: In a Dutch oven or large saucepan, over high heat, bring 8 cups water to rolling boil. Reduce heat to medium. Add 1 tablespoon olive oil, 1 teaspoon kosher salt, and the farfalle pasta to the water. Stir a few times to keep the pasta from sticking together. Cook until pasta is al dente on the edges but still hard in the middle. Remove from heat. Strain. Pour pasta into prepared baking pan, distributing it evenly across entire pan. Set aside.

Cook the peppers and garlic: Heat the remaining 2 tablespoons olive oil, jalapeños, and garlic in medium saucepan over medium-high heat. Stir frequently to ensure peppers are evenly coated with oil. Once the peppers' edges are lightly browned and garlic turns golden brown, add chipotle peppers. Cook for 30 seconds, then remove from heat. Scrape entire mixture into a blender or food processor. Use the "stir" or "chop" setting until mixture turns into a smooth sauce with no lumps. Pour onto pasta. Gently fold the pepper sauce into the pasta, until evenly distributed.

Make the cream sauce: In a medium saucepan, melt the butter over medium heat. Add flour and stir until a grainy, yellowish paste is created. Add milk. Stir constantly for several minutes until the sauce noticeably begins to thicken. Add cheddar cheese and stir until melted. Stir in remaining 2 teaspoons salt. Pour the cream sauce onto the pasta-peppers mixture. Gently stir cream sauce into the pasta until it is evenly distributed.

Bake: Cover the baking pan with aluminum foil, shiny side down. Place in center of the oven and bake, covered, for 20 minutes. Remove foil. Bake uncovered for 10 minutes. Remove from oven. Let stand for 5 minutes. Serve.

Makes 4–6 servings.

SPAGHETTI & MEATBALLS

CONTRIBUTED BY GEROME HUERTA

Saturday may be alright for fighting, but so is Friday when this dish is the main course at Friday Night Dinner. Something about it turns normal conversations about celebrity hair colors and noses into loud affairs, complete with flailing arms and Rory and Lorelai calling each other "nuts" and "double nuts," respectively (which seems backward, doesn't it? Lorelai has definitely earned the "double" title over Rory).

If you've been suffering from ho-hum dinners, try serving this. It may add some zip to dinner conversation! Of course, it may also result in you having to ask the maid-of-the-day to clear everyone's plate after only a few bites.

Sauce:

4	Garlic cloves, crushed or equivalent previously crushed fresh garlic
1 c	Chopped, de-stemmed white mushrooms
¼ c	Minced white onion
2 t	Olive oil
2	29-oz cans tomato sauce
2	8-oz can tomato sauce, no salt added
1 c	Red wine, table or cooking quality
1 c	Cottage cheese
2 T	Dried basil
2 T	Dried oregano
4 t	Dried parsley
1 t	Black pepper (or to taste, adds subtle heat)
¼–½ c	Sugar (or to taste)
	Salt, to taste

Meatballs:

½ lb	Ground, lean sirloin (turkey works too)
½ lb	Sweet Italian sausage, tubing removed (turkey works too)
1	Egg
½ c	Grated Parmesan cheese
2 T	Minced white onion
2 T	Dried Italian seasoning
1 t	Garlic powder or granulated garlic
	Salt and pepper, to taste
½ c	Italian bread crumbs
1 t	Olive oil
1 c	Sauce, prepared, from this recipe

To serve:

	Prepared pasta (spaghetti or angel hair recommended)
	Grated, fresh Parmesan, for sprinkling

Make sauce: In a large saucepan, deep frying pan, or Dutch oven, over medium-high heat, sauté garlic, mushrooms, and onion with olive oil, until onion and garlic are soft and translucent. Add tomato sauces, red wine, cottage cheese, basil, oregano, parsley, and black pepper. Simmer over medium-low heat for 20 minutes, stirring occasionally. Mix in sugar and salt, to taste. Remove from heat and set aside.

Roll meatballs: In a large bowl, combine ground sirloin, sausage, egg, Parmesan, onion, seasonings, and bread crumbs. Mix with hands until fully combined and ingredients are evenly distributed. Using hands, roll meatballs approximately the size of golf balls, not much larger.

Fry meatballs: In a deep frying pan or Dutch oven, over medium-high heat, heat olive oil for 2–3 minutes. Carefully place meatballs in pan with olive oil (oil may splatter). Cover. Cook thoroughly for 10–15 minutes, rotating the meatballs often so they cook evenly. Using a slotted spoon or tongs, remove meatballs from pan and add them to the prepared sauce. Simmer on low heat for 10 minutes.

Serve: Serve over your favorite spaghetti or angel hair pasta. Top with grated, fresh Parmesan.

Makes 4 servings.

CHICKEN & NOODLE CASSEROLE
CONTRIBUTED BY TONY ESCARCEGA

Richard Gilmore spent seven seasons traveling for work, taking conference calls, scoring deals, and bagging Swedes. His "work" was virtually his entire life. So much so, that during the brief time when he wasn't working, he had no idea how to spend his time. What did he do? He went back to work.

Fans came to know his character as the polished and proper Yale grad-turned-successful businessman, in a bow tie. Then, all of a sudden, in the midst of Season 3, Richard showed us he knows how to cook! Well, this one dish at least. It's what his gran would make for him when he was a boy.

Now's your chance to try some of Richard's specialty! Just remember, there are no tiny portions allowed. Big, heaping portions are mandatory. Wearing a bow tie is optional.

2 lbs	Skinless, boneless chicken breast
	Water
¼ t	Salt
1 lb	Dried pasta, rotini recommended
4 T	Butter, divided
1	Yellow onion, diced
1	Carrot, peeled and sliced into ¼-inch thick rounds
1	Zucchini squash, sliced into ¼-inch thick rounds
1	Yellow squash, sliced into ¼-inch thick rounds
1 c	Broccoli crowns, chopped into 1-inch pieces
3 cans	Cream of mushroom soup
1 c	Whole milk
½ c	Half-and-half
1 c	Sour cream
1 T	Fresh thyme
	Salt and pepper, to taste
1 c	Shredded Mexican blend cheese (may substitute ½ c Monterey Jack and ½ c mild cheddar)

Boil chicken: Place chicken in a Dutch oven. Add enough water to just cover the chicken. Bring to a boil over medium-high heat. Boil for 10 minutes. Drain water. Remove chicken from the pot. Cut into 1-inch cubes. Set aside.

Cook pasta: In a Dutch oven or large saucepan, bring water to a boil over medium-high heat. Add salt, then add pasta. Stir. Cook 7–8 minutes only. Pasta will still be very firm in the center. Use a strainer to drain the water. Set aside.

Prep oven: Place oven rack in center position. Preheat oven to 350°F.

Sauté vegetables: In a deep frying pan or Dutch oven, melt 2 tablespoons butter over medium heat. Add onion and sauté for 2–3 minutes. Add carrot. Sauté for additional 2–3 minutes. Add zucchini, yellow squash, and broccoli. Sauté, stirring often, for 5 minutes. Remove from heat and set aside.

Make sauce: In a Dutch oven, melt remaining 2 tablespoons butter over medium heat. Add mushroom soup, milk, half-and-half, sour cream, and thyme. Stir together. Season with salt and pepper, to taste. Simmer on low heat for 10 minutes.

Assemble and bake: To the sauce, add chicken, vegetables, and pasta. Gently stir until combined. Pour mixture into 9x13-inch pan. Cover with shredded cheese. Cover with foil and bake for 15 minutes. Remove foil. Bake for 10 minutes. Remove from oven. Serve hot.

Makes 8–10 servings.

PAELLA

TOWN FAVORITE

Logan's visit to Stars Hollow was destined to be a turning point in his relationship with Lorelai. Between bringing the orchids and cooking paella, Logan put on his most charming act for her. And it worked! Long after dinner, during their impromptu talk in the middle of the night, over pie, she finally told him her concerns and gave him a chance to sway her view of him and earn her respect.

Take a lesson from Logan, the master charmer: serve this when you are trying to get in someone's good graces. Don't forget the orchids!

½ c	Flat-leaf parsley
½ c	Curly-leaf parsley
1 c	Lemon juice, freshly squeezed, divided
4 T	Olive oil, divided
6–7	Garlic cloves, minced
4	Boneless, skinless chicken thighs, halved
½ lb	Chorizo sausage, ground or cut into ½-inch slices
12	Jumbo shrimp, deveined
2 c	Homemade Chicken Broth (see page 93), or low-sodium packaged broth
1	Medium sweet yellow onion
2	Jalapeño peppers, stems removed, thinly sliced
3	Roma tomatoes
½ t	Kosher salt
½ t	Black pepper
120	Saffron threads (about 1 g)
2 c	Arborio rice
1 c	Water, warm

Season chicken: In a medium bowl or a gallon zip lock bag, combine both parsleys, ½ cup of lemon juice, 2 tablespoons olive oil, and garlic. Add chicken thigh pieces, and either stir or shake to coat. Set aside, at room temperature.

Cook chorizo: Add 1 tablespoon olive oil to a deep frying pan or paella pan, over medium heat. Add chorizo. Cook for 4–5 minutes, stirring often. Remove chorizo from pan and set aside.

Cook chicken: In the same frying pan, add the seasoned chicken to the chorizo oils (don't discard the seasoning mix—you'll need it later in this recipe). Fry chicken for 2 minutes per side. Remove chicken from pan and set aside.

Cook shrimp: Add shrimp to same frying pan. Over medium heat, cook shrimp for 1 minute per side. Remove shrimp and set aside.

Warm broth: In a separate, medium saucepan, simmer broth over medium heat for 10 minutes.

Make paella: Using the same frying/paella pan, heat the remaining olive oil over medium heat. Add the onion, jalapeños, and tomatoes. Sauté for 3 minutes. Add the lemon-and-garlic mixture. Add salt, pepper, and saffron. Add rice. Stir until combined. Add the warm broth and water. Add meats. Cook, stirring every 2–3 minutes, until rice becomes al dente. Remove from heat. Let stand for 10 minutes. Serve.

Makes 6–8 servings.

Appetizers & Side Dishes

SALMON PUFFS

EMILY'S HOUSE

Every one of Emily's events features Salmon Puffs—so either she really likes salmon, or it's the one dish she gets the most compliments on. Odds are, it's the latter.

These little puffs really are a great option for your next party. They look fancy and taste great; they are easy to make, and cleanup is quick. If you're worried about whether or not your guests like salmon, just remember, everything tastes better in a puff.

½–⅔ c	**Fresh, skinned salmon**
¾ t	**Fresh dill**
¼ c	**Lemon juice, freshly squeezed**
¼ t	**Cayenne pepper**
1 t	**Grainy deli-style mustard**
4 t	**Port Salut cheese, rind removed**
	Flour, for dusting
2	**Puff pastry sheets**
	Chives for garnish, cut into 90 1-inch pieces

Prepare oven: Preheat oven to 400°F. Move rack to center position.

Mix salmon filling: In a food processor, add salmon, dill, lemon juice, and cayenne pepper. Process until a coarse paste forms. Add mustard and cheese. Process until the mixture is smooth. Set aside.

Cut dough: Lay out a sheet of puff pastry on a lightly floured work surface. Use a shot glass (or any round cutter that is 2-inches in diameter) to cut 15 circles from the sheet.

Assemble: Using a mini muffin pan or tart pan, press a round of dough into each cup. Use a small fork to poke 10–15 holes into the bottom/flat part of the dough. Put the salmon mixture into a pastry bag with a wide-gauge tip, or a zip-locking bag with the corner trimmed off. Squeeze about 1 teaspoon of the mixture into the center of each cup.

Bake, garnish, and serve: Bake puffs for 12 minutes. Remove from oven. Salmon may have popped up during baking. If so, press it back down into pastry. Remove puffs to a plate or serving platter. Use a skewer or two toothpicks to make a hole, ¼-inch deep, in the center of each puff. Place 3 pieces of chive into the hole, so they are sticking straight up. Serve.

Makes 30 puffs.

Tester—Melissa McAndrews

FRIED STUFFED SQUASH BLOSSOMS

Depending where you live, finding squash blossoms to stuff may be challenging. Just like the time Jackson suggested Sookie try stuffing something else, you may feel tempted to do the same. But Sookie's customers are obsessed with these for a reason—they're light, crunchy, delicious little packets of cheesy goodness. Grocers don't usually carry them, so try your local farmers market, Asian market, or grow some squash in the backyard. You'll be happy you did!

	Vegetable oil
1 c	Ricotta cheese
½ c	Mascarpone cheese
¼ t	Kosher salt
½ t	Black pepper
2 T	Fresh, chopped basil
½ c	Flour
3 oz	Lager beer
¼ lb	Squash blossoms (about 15), washed
	Marinara Sauce, ¼ batch from page 148–149 or jarred, for serving

Heat oil: Add vegetable oil to a Dutch oven until the oil is 3-inches deep. Insert a candy thermometer. Bring to 325°F over high heat.

Prep cooling racks: Place 1–2 cooling racks on work surface, with paper towels beneath each. Set aside.

Mix filling: In a medium bowl, combine cheeses, salt, pepper, and basil. Stir until fully combined.

Mix batter: In a shallow bowl, add flour. Pour beer onto flour, and whisk until combined. Set aside.

Pipe filling into blossoms: Fill a pastry bag or a zip-locking bag with cheese mixture. Cut tip off pastry bag or corner off plastic bag. Gently open each blossom and pipe 1 teaspoon of mixture into each. Gently twist the top of each blossom closed, so cheese won't ooze out during the cooking process.

Batter blossoms: Carefully drag each side of each blossom through batter. Once blossom is fully battered, carefully add it to the oil using a slotted spoon. Fry for 1–2 minutes per side, turning once. Once blossom has a light, golden brown crust on the outside, remove it from the oil. Place on a cooling rack. Cool for 2 minutes. Serve with marinara sauce.

Makes about 15 blossoms.

ROQUEFORT PUFFS

These were served at the funeral for "Cinnamon," the cat Babette and Morey rolled around town in a custom-made cat wagon and then lost to old age. The funeral was potluck-style. Sookie brought these; Luke brought burgers and fries. Who knows what kind of food anyone else brought, but there's a good chance folks went home with very confused bellies that night.

It's clear why Sookie chose these. They're easy to make, easy to transport, and a real crowd-pleaser. The puffy outside gives way to the sharp tang of the cheesy center, making folks reach for a second one even before they've finished their first.

You don't have to wait for a cat funeral to make these. They'll be a welcome addition at any gathering.

1½ c	Mascarpone
6 T	Heavy cream
8 oz	Roquefort cheese
	Flour, for dusting
2	Puff pastry sheets, room temperature

Prep oven and pan: Place oven rack in center position. Preheat oven to 425°F. Cover a cookie sheet with parchment paper. Set aside.

Make filling: In a medium bowl, mix mascarpone and heavy cream. Crumble Roquefort into the mix. Stir until fully combined.

Cut pastry: Lightly flour a work surface. Lay out one sheet of puff pastry. Using a pastry cutter, pizza cutter, or knife, cut the sheet into 12 equal pieces (squares if possible). Cut each piece diagonally into two triangles. This will result in 24 triangles. Repeat steps with second puff pastry sheet.

Bake pastry: Place as many pastry triangles as possible on cookie sheet. Bake for 12 minutes. Triangles should be puffed up. Remove from oven.

Pipe filling: Fill a pastry bag or a zip-locking bag with cheese mixture. Cut tip off pastry bag or corner off plastic bag. Gently insert the tip of the bag into the cut side of each puff and pipe approximately ½ teaspoon of mixture into each.

Bake puffs: Return filled puffs to baking tray. Place in oven and bake for 2 minutes. Remove. Cool for 2 minutes. Serve.

Makes 48 puffs.

MUSHROOM CAPS

EMILY'S HOUSE

For years after Richard and Emily fronted the money for Chilton, Lorelai felt weighed down by the obligation of having to go to Friday Night Dinner, every, single, week. So once she repaid the debt, and the weight was lifted, you'd think she and Rory would have planned some big, fun junk food fest for their first Friday night out of confinement. Nope. They sat on their sofa, bored, dreaming of the Mushroom Caps being served at the party Richard and Emily hosted that night. (Were the elder Gilmores celebrating the end of Friday Night Dinners?) Next time you're celebrating your freedom from something odious, this is the dish to serve.

3 T	Olive oil, divided
1	Large shallot, minced
2 oz	Pancetta, chopped
½ c + 2 T	Marsala wine, divided
1	Garlic clove, large, minced
14–16	Large white or cremini mushrooms, stems removed
1	Egg
⅔ c	Panko bread crumbs
1 t	Minced flat-leaf parsley
½ t	Balsamic vinegar
¼ t	Kosher salt
¼ t	Black pepper
½ c	Mascarpone cheese
	Additional chopped flat-leaf parsley, for garnish

Prep oven and pan: Place oven rack in center position. Preheat oven to 350°F. Cover the bottom of a cookie sheet with parchment paper. Set aside.

Cook garlic and pancetta: In a medium frying pan, over medium-high heat, combine 1 tablespoon olive oil, shallot, and pancetta. Cook 5 minutes, stirring often, until pancetta becomes crisp and most of the oil has been absorbed. Remove from pan using a slotted spoon and place in a medium mixing bowl. Set aside.

Cook mushrooms: In the same frying pan, over medium heat, combine 2 tablespoons olive oil, 2 tablespoons Marsala wine, and garlic. Cook 2 minutes, stirring once. Add mushrooms. Turn them regularly to cook them evenly. Cook them until they start to give water and both sides are golden brown. Remove each mushroom individually, and place them on a paper towel to absorb excess liquids.

Make filling: Into the bowl containing the pancetta, add the egg, panko, parsley, balsamic vinegar, salt, and pepper. Use hands to work the ingredients together and distribute them evenly.

Fill mushrooms: Use a teaspoon to fill each mushroom. The amount used to fill will vary based on the size of each mushroom. The inside of each mushroom should be completely filled, and a rounded mound of filling should stick up over the mushroom about ¼ inch. Place each filled mushroom onto the prepared baking pan. Set aside.

Make sauce: Reheat the pan the mushrooms were cooked in, over medium-high heat for 1–2 minutes. Add ½ cup of Marsala wine and, as it's bubbling, use a spatula to scrape any bits from the bottom of the pan (in other words, deglaze the pan). Add mascarpone and melt, stirring often so the cheese and wine combine into a tan-colored sauce. Once all cheese is melted, spoon ¼–½ teaspoon of sauce onto each mushroom—use more sauce for bigger mushrooms. Use enough sauce to moisten all of the filling in each mushroom.

Bake mushroom caps: Place tray in oven, on the center rack. Bake for 15–18 minutes, until the filling in each mushroom has developed a crunchy top. Remove. Let cool for 2 minutes. Garnish with parsley, if desired. Serve.

Makes 14–16 mushroom caps.

DEVILED EGGS

TOWN FAVORITE

Throughout the series, Lorelai and Rory show us they know how to put their own feelings aside, in order to do something nice or supportive for people they love. A clear example of their ability to rise above was Sherry's baby shower. A few short months after suffering the disappointment of Chris leaving Lorelai, again, they both attended and participated. Granted, Lorelai had a mini fit in the bathroom. But, overall, they put on a good act.

Afterward, they let their bottled-up anger fly, when they pelted Jess's car with leftover Deviled Eggs.

One aspect of this story is slightly far-fetched, though. There's no way any Deviled Eggs were left over. See for yourself—serve these and watch them disappear.

12	**Eggs**
	Water
2 T	**Mustard**
2 T	**Mayonnaise**
3 T	**Sour cream**
1 T	**Dill relish**
¼ t	**Kosher salt**
¼ t	**Black pepper**
¼ t	**Cayenne pepper**
	Paprika, for garnish

Boil eggs: Place eggs in a large saucepan or Dutch oven. Fill pan with water just until eggs are covered. Place pan on burner over medium-high heat. Bring to a boil. Boil for 8 minutes. Remove from heat. Let eggs remain in the hot water for 5 minutes. Drain hot water from pan. Fill pan with cold water and let sit for 2–3 minutes. Repeat, continuing to fill/drain pan until eggs are cool to the touch. Then crack and peel each egg. Carefully cut each egg in half, lengthwise. Remove the cooked yolks and place them in a small mixing bowl.

Make filling: To the bowl containing the egg yolks, add mustard, mayonnaise, sour cream, dill relish, salt, black pepper, and cayenne pepper. Combine ingredients using a hand mixer or a fork.

Fill eggs: Fill a pastry bag or a zip-locking bag with yolk mixture. Cut tip off pastry bag or corner off plastic bag. With a steady hand, hold the tip of the bag right over the rounded-out part of each egg and pipe filling until it comes up, over the edge. Lightly sprinkle each egg with paprika. Serve.

Makes 24 Deviled Eggs.

BRUSCHETTA

RORY COOKS

During the seven years of the series, Rory grows from a shy, awkward bookish girl into an accomplished, confident woman. We watch as she subconsciously decides which aspects of her upbringing to carry with her into adulthood and which aspects to discard. During Season 6, we see her begin to dabble in something rather shocking and very out of character—cooking! Maybe it's Logan's influence or maybe she's satisfying her own curiosity (she showed a spark of this when she made dinner for Dean), but yes, we see Rory cook.

This is the perfect dish for a beginner, like Rory—there is very little actual "cooking" required and the results are delicious. If you're trying your hand in the kitchen for the first time, make this. If you're cooking for the millionth time and just want something fresh and tasty to serve your weekend guests, make this.

1	Baguette
4	Roma tomatoes, large, diced
¼ c	Chopped, fresh basil
5–6	Garlic cloves, peeled and minced
1 T	Balsamic vinegar
2 T	Olive oil
½ t	Black pepper
½ t	Kosher salt
1 t	Dried oregano
1 T	Lemon juice, freshly squeezed
1 t	Lemon zest

Prep oven and pan: Place oven rack in center position. Preheat oven to 300°F. Get out a cookie sheet.

Toast bread: Using a serrated knife, slice baguette into ½-inch slices. Place each slice on its side, on the cookie sheet. Place cookie sheet in the oven for 15 minutes. Bread should be toasted and crispy but not browned. Remove pan from oven and set aside to cool.

Make topping: In a medium bowl, combine tomatoes, basil, garlic, vinegar, and olive oil. Toss ingredients together. Add pepper, salt, oregano, lemon juice, and lemon zest. Toss again, just enough to combine.

Assemble: Use a spoon to top each baguette slice with a generous portion of tomato mixture. Serve.

Makes about 24 bruschetta portions, depending on baguette.

BEEF SKEWERS

Is this an appetizer? Or is this a main course? Since the show posed the question but never supplied the answer, it's up to you to decide. If you cannot choose, ask your valet's opinion. Just don't serve it as both.

1 lb	Top sirloin beef
4	Large garlic cloves, smashed
1 t	Allspice berries
2 t	Black peppercorns
1 t	Crushed red pepper
1 t	Kosher salt
¼ c	Olive oil
¼ c	Red wine vinegar
1 c	Water

Note: *If you are using wooden skewers, place them into a shallow pan and cover them with water overnight before making this dish.*

Marinate meat: Using a sharp knife, cut beef into strips that are 1x1-inch around and 4–5-inches long. Trim all fat off. Place meat into a large zip-locking bag. Add garlic, allspice, peppercorns, red pepper, salt, olive oil, vinegar, and water. Zip bag closed. (If you don't have a bag, place beef and marinade in a small mixing bowl and cover with plastic wrap). Refrigerate for 1 hour.

Prepare oven: Turn on broiler. If your broiler is in your oven, place the oven rack on the top rung. Find a large, shallow pan—this could be a cookie sheet with edges on it or a 9x13-inch metal baking pan (do NOT use a glass pan for broiling). Line the bottom of the pan with a large piece of aluminum foil, shiny side up. Place wire cooling rack(s) into the pan.

Broil skewers: Insert a skewer into each piece of meat, lengthwise, so the skewer reaches nearly to the other end of the beef. Place each beef skewer on the wire rack inside the pan. Place pan in broiler for 4 minutes. Remove pan, carefully flip skewers to the other side, and return pan to broiler for 4 additional minutes. Remove pan from broiler. Use an oven mitt or hot pad to transfer skewers from pan to serving plate. Serve.

Makes 5–6 beef skewers.

RATATOUILLE

Dear Sookie is so loyal to Jackson, as both a wife and as a customer, that when another produce supplier drops off a sample basket filled with vegetables, she keeps the whole thing a secret. Sure, the chef in her was reeled in by the gorgeousness of the produce; it seduced her into making the best Ratatouille of her life. But once Jackson popped in, the Ratatouille went into the bin and Jackson was none the wiser. That's love.

This recipe requires several steps, but it's worth the effort. The final result will entice even the most "I don't like vegetables" member of your crew.

7 T	Olive oil, divided
1	Sweet yellow onion, coarsely chopped
½ c	Cubed red pepper
½ c	Cubed yellow pepper
3 c	Cubed eggplant
1 t	Dried herbes de Provence
3 c	Cubed zucchini
½ t	Kosher salt, plus extra to taste
3	Garlic cloves, minced
3 c	Cubed, de-stemmed white or cremini mushrooms
½ c	Dry white wine (chardonnay recommended)
3 c	Cubed tomatoes
2 T	Fresh, minced basil
1 T	Fresh, minced thyme
½ t	Ground black pepper
1 T	Fresh, minced parsley for garnish

Sauté onion, pepper, and eggplant: Heat 4 tablespoons olive oil in a Dutch oven, over medium-high heat for 2 minutes. Add onion, peppers, and eggplant. Sprinkle with herbes de Provence. Sauté, stirring occasionally with a spatula or wooden spoon, for 4–5 minutes, until eggplant begins to show browning on the edges and onions are translucent. Transfer to a large bowl and set aside.

Sauté zucchini: Using the same Dutch oven, same spatula/spoon, heat 1 tablespoon olive oil over medium-high heat for 2 minutes. Add zucchini. Sprinkle with ½ teaspoon kosher salt. Sauté, stirring occasionally, until the zucchini has shed its water and its edges show the first signs of browning, about 4–5 minutes. Transfer it to the bowl with the eggplant and peppers. Set aside.

Sauté mushrooms and garlic: Returning to the Dutch oven, over medium-high heat, warm the remaining 2 tablespoons olive oil for 2 minutes. Add garlic and mushrooms. Sauté for 3–4 minutes. Watch for the mushrooms to shed their water—then continue to sauté for about a minute. Transfer to the same bowl with the zucchini. Set aside.

Deglaze Dutch oven and make Ratatouille: Over medium-high heat, place the Dutch oven back on the stove for 1 minute. Pour the wine into the pot, let it sizzle a bit, then use a spatula or wooden spoon to scrape any cooking scraps off the bottom of the pan (this is deglazing). Add the vegetables back into the pot. Add tomatoes. Fold in basil and thyme. Sprinkle with black pepper. Add Kosher salt, to taste. Slowly and carefully stir the mixture to blend. Cover and simmer over low heat for 15 minutes. Spoon into bowls or onto plates. Sprinkle with parsley. Serve.

Makes 4 main dish servings or 8 side dish servings.

Tester—Shelby Sloan

Eat Like a Gilmore

MASHED POTATOES

LUKE'S DINER

Mashed Potatoes appear everywhere in Gilmore Land—at Friday Night Dinner, at the inns, even at the dinner Rory cooked for Dean during Donna Reed night. So it was difficult to choose who to attribute this dish to. Considering he served Lorelai Mashed Potatoes for breakfast, as a cold remedy, Luke won.

You can make the basic recipe to top with gravy, or go full Sookie by adding the optional ingredients. Either way, this dish will cure your urge for comfort food.

3 lbs	Potatoes, any type, skins on or peeled
	Water
1 t	Kosher salt
½ c	Butter, room temperature
⅔ c	Whole milk or half-and-half, room temperature
½ t	Cayenne pepper, optional
1 c	Grated Romano cheese, optional
	Salt and pepper, to taste

Boil potatoes: Cut potatoes into uniform 2-inch pieces. Place them in a large saucepan. Fill the pan with just enough water to cover the potatoes. Add kosher salt. Cover. Bring to a boil over medium-high heat. Reduce heat to medium. Simmer for 12–15 minutes. Check doneness by inserting a fork into a piece of potato. If you feel any resistance, continue cooking. Once the fork slides in smoothly, remove from heat. Drain water.

Mash potatoes: Place potatoes in a large mixing bowl (or you can do this right in the pan). Use a hand mixer on medium low speed to "mash" the potatoes. Add butter, milk, cayenne pepper, Romano cheese, and salt and pepper to taste. Continue to mix until potatoes reach the consistency you desire. Scoop potatoes into a serving bowl. Serve.

Makes 6–8 servings.

PANCETTA CHESTNUT STUFFING

Sookie really is the best chef, hands down (don't say "one of" or we'll never get out of here). She puts an artistic, creative spin on everything she makes—even traditional dishes, like stuffing. In fact, each holiday meal at her house is probably completely new and different from the year before. How fun!

If your family has been making the same stuffing recipe since the disco era, try jazzing up your holiday table by serving this instead.

8 c	Cubed ciabatta bread, in ½-inch pieces
2 T	Olive oil
3	Shallots, large, peeled, minced
3	Garlic cloves
8 oz	Pancetta, chopped
3	Celery stalks, diced
2	Carrots, peeled and diced
1½ t	Fresh thyme
1½ t	Fresh rosemary
¾ c	Prunes
2	Eggs
¾ c	Homemade Chicken Broth (see page 93), or low-sodium packaged broth
¾ c	Vacuum-packed, peeled and roasted chestnuts
1 t	Fresh parsley
1 T	Grated Parmesan cheese

Prep oven: Place the oven rack in the center position. Preheat oven to 375°F.

Toast bread: Arrange bread cubes in a single layer on a cookie sheet. Place in oven for 15 minutes. Bread will be toasted and crispy, but not browned. Remove and set aside.

Sauté pancetta and vegetables: In a deep frying pan, add olive oil, shallots, garlic, and pancetta. Sauté over medium heat for 5 minutes. Add celery and carrots. Continue to sauté for 5 minutes. Add thyme, rosemary, and prunes. Continue to sauté for 3 minutes. Remove from heat. Bring to room temperature.

Make stuffing: In a large (ideally oven-safe) bowl, beat eggs. Add bread and sautéed vegetables. Mix. Add chicken broth, chestnuts, parsley, and Parmesan. Mix until ingredients are evenly distributed. If bowl is oven-safe, use it. If bowl is not oven-safe, grease a baking pan and transfer stuffing into it. Cover with aluminum foil, shiny side down. Place inside oven and bake for 15 minutes. Remove aluminum foil. Bake for 7–10 minutes. Once the top tips turn dark golden brown and crispy, remove. Let cool for 5 minutes. Serve.

Makes 8–10 servings.

WARM POTATO & CHORIZO SALAD

CONTRIBUTED BY TONY ESCARCEGA

As the healthy part of the guilt dinner Sookie prepares for Jackson, this salad is . . . not that healthy. But it is a unique, combination of flavors—the kind only a talented chef would think to combine. It's perfectly enhanced by the light, spicy, citrus dressing. The next time you want a salad, but your partner wants meat and potatoes, serve this. It'll satisfy both cravings.

1 lb	Red or new potatoes, cleaned, quartered
	Water
1 T	Salt
¾ lb	Chorizo, ground or with casings removed
1 lb	Asparagus tips, cut into 2-inch pieces
½ lb	De-stemmed spinach, washed
	Shredded Parmesan cheese, for serving

Dressing:

1 c	Lime juice, freshly squeezed
½ c	Cilantro leaves
1 c	Sour cream
¼ c	Mayonnaise
2	Jalapeños, coarsely chopped (double this if you like a lot of heat)

Boil potatoes: Place quartered potatoes into a Dutch oven. Fill with just enough water to cover potatoes. Bring to a boil over medium-high heat. Cover and cook until tender, roughly 15 minutes. Drain. Cover and set aside.

Cook chorizo: Place chorizo in a deep frying pan. Over medium-high heat, cook until meat turns brownish red. Add cut asparagus to pan. Sauté for 5–7 minutes, until asparagus becomes tender (but not soft). Remove from heat.

Make Dressing: In a blender or food processor, combine lime juice, cilantro, sour cream, mayonnaise, and jalapeño. Blend until ingredients combine to form a liquid. Pour into a serving pitcher, gravy boat, or serving bowl.

Mix salad: In a large serving bowl, mix spinach, potatoes, and chorizo/asparagus mixture. Serve, with dressing on the side and shredded Parmesan cheese.

Makes 6–8 servings.

Meats, Seafood
& Main Dishes

POT ROAST

EMILY'S HOUSE

Pot Roast: it's a quintessentially welcoming, "family" meal, isn't it? Not at the Gilmores'. Pot Roast is the meal Emily served for Rory, causing Rory to ask, "Am I dying?" Rory was wise to look for an ulterior motive. But, no, Rory, wasn't dying. Rory was just being baited to join a conversation with the good Reverend Boatwright, who had been called in to interrogate her about her sex life with Logan.

That's the power of the Pot Roast—even Rory, wise to her grandmother's ways, suspicious she was being trapped, still sat down to dinner.

Now you have the recipe. Use your power wisely.

Pot Roast:

2 lb	Chuck roast (may be labeled "Pot Roast")— flat, quality cut of meat
2 t	Kosher salt
1 t	Black pepper
½ c	Olive oil, divided
2 T	Butter, divided
½	Yellow onion, cut in wide half-slices
2	Garlic cloves, minced
3	Carrots, peeled, and cut wide slices
3	Celery stalks, trimmed and cut in wide slices
8	Red or new potatoes, quartered
3	Beef bouillon cubes
⅔ c	Red wine
2 c	Water
1 T	Fresh parsley
1 T	Fresh thyme

Gravy:

2 c	Skimmed and strained pan juices
2 T	Cornstarch
2 T	Cold water

Prep meat: Pat meat dry and rub 1 teaspoon kosher salt plus ½ teaspoon black pepper onto each side. Set aside.

Brown vegetables: In a Dutch oven, heat ¼ cup olive oil and 1 tablespoon butter over medium-high heat for 2 minutes. Add onion, garlic, carrots, celery, and potatoes. Use a spatula or wooden spoon to move the pieces around to coat each one with oil/butter. Cook for 5–6 minutes, stirring occasionally. Once the onions are translucent and potatoes begin to show browning, use a slotted spoon to remove all pieces from the pot. Set aside.

Sear meat: Add the remaining oil and butter to the pot. Apply high heat for 2 minutes. Carefully add meat. Oil may bubble up a little or pop—so take a step back. Cook for 2 minutes per side. While it's cooking, press the meat up against the side of the pot to sear the sides, as well. Remove meat and set aside.

Simmer Pot Roast: Smash up the bouillon a little and put it in the pot. Turn the heat to high and use the oil remaining in the pot to dissolve it. Add wine and water. Bring to a boil. Reduce heat. Add meat back into the pot, then vegetables. Add parsley and thyme. If the liquid does not fully cover the meat and veggies, add just enough water to cover. Cover the pot with a tight lid. Cook on very low heat for 1 hour. When meat thermometer reads 200°F, the meat is cooked and can be served. However, I like to leave the pot cooking at a very low temperature for 30–90 minutes more to make the meat very tender.

Plate the meat and prepare remaining liquids: Using a meat fork or two large forks, remove the meat and place in the center of a platter or large plate. Using a slotted spoon, remove the vegetables and place them around the meat. Skim fat from the remaining liquids; discard fat. Strain liquids into a bowl to remove any remaining bits. Return liquids to pot.

Make Gravy: In a small bowl or jar, combine cornstarch and water. Mix until it turns into a smooth, runny paste, free from lumps. Mix the paste into the liquids in the pot. Over medium-high heat, continue to stir the liquids until they thicken, about 4–5 minutes. This is your gravy. Pour into a serving vessel. Serve.

Makes 4–6 servings.

Tester—Nicky Krieger-Loos

Eat Like a Gilmore

LAMB CHOPS WITH OLIVES, ROSEMARY & GARLIC

Many people made references to Lamb Chops during the course of the series. So much so, it seems possible one of the writers may have had a thing for Lamb Chops. However, no one's sounded more enticing than the ones Sookie served at the guilt meal (not to be confused with a rant meal) she made for Jackson. "Lamb Chops" was the star of the night.

Once you make these, it'll be easy to see why Sookie chose this dish. Not only do the ingredients combine to make a savory sauce that perfectly complements the tender meat, its aromas make the whole house smell like an Italian grandmother is running your kitchen. Try it—you'll see how Jackson was lulled into forgiveness.

2	Lamb loin chops, ½ lb each
1 t	Kosher salt
1 t	Pepper
½ c	Olive oil, divided
½	Red onion, thinly sliced
4	Garlic cloves, minced
½ c	Dry white wine (chardonnay or similar)
1 T	Tomato paste
½ c	Water
8	Green olives, large, pitted, halved
4	Fresh rosemary sprigs

Prepare oven and lamb chops: Preheat oven to 375°F. Rub lamb chops with salt and pepper: ¼ teaspoon salt and ¼ teaspoon pepper on each side of each chop. Set aside.

Cook onions and garlic: Heat ¼ cup olive oil in a deep frying pan. Add onion and garlic, and cook until onions are translucent. Remove from heat. Use onion-garlic mixture to coat the bottom of a small, shallow baking dish. Return frying pan to the stove.

Sear lamb chops: Over medium-high heat, add ¼ cup olive oil. Add lamb chops and sear for 2 minutes on each side. Remove the chops from heat, and place them on top of the onion-garlic mixture in the baking dish. Return frying pan to stove.

Make sauce: Over medium-high heat, add wine to the pan. Heat the wine and use a spatula to scrape any cooked bits from the bottom of the pan. Add the tomato paste and stir until dissolved. Stir in water. Heat the sauce for 3 minutes, stirring occasionally. Remove from heat. Pour sauce over lamb chops.

Bake lamb chops: Add olives and rosemary to baking dish. Cover. Cook for 10 minutes. Turn chops. Cook for an additional 10 minutes.

Serve: To serve, spoon sauce over meat and top with the olives. Add a piece of the roasted rosemary for garnish.

Makes 2 servings.

Tester—Shannon Huffman

FRIED CHICKEN & FRIED CHICKEN SUSHI

SOOKIE'S KITCHEN

What happens when you combine the creativity of a master chef like Sookie with the creativity of a master nut like Lorelai? Fried Chicken Sushi.

So while Luke made Fried Chicken earlier in the show, this Sookie/Lorelai brainstorm yielded one of the greatest culinary ideas in its entire run. Make the Fried Chicken any time the mood strikes. Make the sushi version whenever you need to recreate Asia in your living room.

	Vegetable oil
1	Egg
2 c	Buttermilk
1 T	Hot sauce (Frank's RedHot®, recommended)
2 c	Flour
2 T	Kosher salt
1½ T	Black pepper
2 T	Smoked paprika
1	Whole chicken, 3–4 lbs, cut into parts, washed and patted dry

For Fried Chicken Sushi:

1½ c	Medium-grain rice
2 c	Water
2 T	Sushi-seasoned rice vinegar
1 c	Thinly sliced red cabbage
1 c	Thinly sliced green cabbage
¼ c	Peeled, finely grated carrot
2 t	Minced chives
1 T	Sesame oil
1 T	Rice vinegar
½ t	Tamarind
½ t	Black pepper
	Seaweed sushi paper
	Pieces of fried chicken
½ c	Mayonnaise
4 t	Sriracha sauce

Heat oil: Add vegetable oil to a Dutch oven until the oil is 3 inches deep. Insert a candy thermometer. Bring to 350°F over high heat.

Prep cooling racks: Place 1–2 cooling racks on work surface, with paper towels beneath each. Set aside.

Make batter: In a medium, shallow bowl, mix egg until yolk and white are fully combined. Add buttermilk and hot sauce. Stir until fully combined.

Batter chicken: In another shallow bowl, combine flour, salt, pepper, and paprika until fully mixed. One by one, place each piece of chicken into the flour mix; flip it and move it around until it's completely coated. Then place it in the batter. Again, flip it around and move it until it is completely coated. Place the batter-coated piece back into the flour mix for a second coat. Then dip it into the batter for a second coat. Place the piece on a plate and allow it to sit for a few minutes. Repeat this for each piece.

Fry chicken: Use tongs to slowly and carefully place the battered chicken pieces into the hot oil. Cook batches of 2–3 pieces at one time. (Having too many pieces in the oil at once will lower the temp of the oil and make your chicken soggy.) Keep the oil temperature between 330°F and 350°F. If the oil gets hotter than 350°F, the outside will burn before the inside is fully cooked. If the oil is too hot, quickly turn down the burner and/or add more oil, ½ cup at a time, until the temperature comes down. To test doneness, insert a meat thermometer. When it reads 160°F, the meat is done. Use tongs to remove each piece and place it on the cooling rack. Repeat until all pieces are cooked. Serve.

Makes 8 pieces.

Make Fried Chicken Sushi:

Cook rice: Rinse and cook rice per package instructions. Fold in sushi-seasoned rice vinegar. Set aside.

Make coleslaw: In a medium bowl combine both cabbages, carrot, chives, sesame oil, rice vinegar, tamarind, and black pepper until blended. Set aside.

Make sushi: Cover half a sheet of seaweed with a thin layer of cooked rice (about 1 cup). Cover the center of rice with a 1–1½ inch layer of coleslaw. Top the coleslaw with cut pieces of fried chicken. Starting with the rice side, roll seaweed into a tube/roll. Use a sharp knife to cut the roll into 6–8 pieces.

Make sauce and serve: Mix mayonnaise with sriracha. Drizzle sauce on sushi pieces or serve sushi pieces with sriracha-mayo as dipping sauce.

Makes 4 servings.

MEATLOAF

Was it Luke's Meatloaf that finally landed Kirk a girlfriend? We don't actually know what Lulu ordered on that fateful dinner date, but we did see him recommend it to her.

She must have ordered it. Because if ever a meatloaf could strike up a romance, this is it. With no ketchup, some cheddar cheese, and a little hot sauce, this isn't your high school cafeteria's mushy meatloaf. This is Luke's Meatloaf, the meatloaf that gets you hot.

2 T	Butter
1 c	Grated yellow onion
3	Minced garlic cloves
⅓ c	Tomato sauce
1 T	Balsamic vinegar
1 T	Hot sauce (Frank's RedHot, recommended)
1	Egg
1 lb	Lean ground beef
⅓ c	Finely grated medium cheddar cheese
⅔ c	Panko bread crumbs
1 t	Dried parsley
1 t	Kosher salt
1 t	Black pepper

Prep oven and pan: Place oven rack in center position. Preheat oven to 350°F. Take out one 8½x4½-inch meatloaf pan. (Two 5¾x3¼-inch mini meatloaf pans may be substituted.) Set aside.

Sauté onion and garlic: In a frying pan, over medium heat, melt butter. Once fully melted, add grated onion and garlic. Sauté for 4–5 minutes, until most of the water has evaporated. Remove from heat and bring to room temperature.

Mix sauce: In a small bowl, combine tomato sauce, balsamic vinegar, and hot sauce. Stir until blended. Set aside.

Mix meatloaf: In a large mixing bowl, mix egg until yolk and white are combined. Add ground beef, cheese, panko, parsley, salt, pepper, and the mixed sauce. Use hands to mix ingredients together. Add onions and garlic. Use hands to mix until all ingredients are fully combined.

Bake meatloaf and serve: Form meatloaf into an oblong ball. Place it into the pan and press it so there are no air bubbles at the bottom of the pan and the top of the meatloaf is flat. Place in oven and bake for 60 minutes. Insert a meat thermometer around the 55-minute mark to test doneness. Meatloaf is done when the inside temperature reaches 160°F. Remove from oven. Let cool for 10 minutes. Slice into 1-inch slabs. Serve.

Makes 4 servings.

LAMB & ARTICHOKE STEW

As the main course for the romantic dinner Luke made for Lorelai, this dish stands out as being unique, yet homey at the same time: perfect for Lorelai.

1 lb	Lamb meat, cubed
½ t	Kosher salt
1 t	Black pepper
2 oz	Pancetta
1 T	Olive oil
½ c	Minced leeks (white part, only)
3	Garlic cloves, minced
½ c	White wine (chardonnay recommended)
4 c	Homemade Chicken Broth (see page 93), or low-sodium packaged broth
½ c	Cool water
3 T	Cornstarch
½ c	Lemon juice, freshly squeezed
1	13–16-oz can artichoke quarters or hearts, drained, chopped
2 T	Chopped mint leaves
1 T	Chopped, fresh oregano
½ t	Crushed red pepper

Season lamb: Coat lamb cubes with salt and black pepper. Set aside.

Sauté meats, leeks, and garlic: In a Dutch oven, over medium-high heat, sauté pancetta for 3–4 minutes until edges start to get crispy. Add olive oil, leeks, garlic, and lamb. Sauté until lamb is browned on all sides.

Make broth: Add wine and chicken broth to the Dutch oven. Bring to a boil. In a cup or small bowl, combine water and cornstarch. Stir until cornstarch fully dissolves. Add water-cornstarch slurry to the pan and stir until fully blended. Continue stirring until broth begins to thicken.

Make stew: Add lemon juice, artichokes, mint, oregano, and red pepper. Stir to combine. Simmer over low heat for 15 minutes. Serve.

Makes 3–4 servings.

ROASTED DUCK
IN A CHOCOLATE ORANGE SAUCE

With an inn full of guests expecting a delectable dinner with duck as its main event, a pregnant Sookie prescribed immediate bed rest, and no capable Sookie stand-in on the kitchen staff, Lorelai had to find a solution—fast. With a calm urgency, she turned on her charm and convinced Luke to step in. Never one to turn down a good hero opportunity, Luke swooped in and saved dinner at the Dragonfly that night—even with Sookie micromanaging him from afar the entire time. Here is your chance to determine your answer to the eternal question posed that night. Will you strain the sauce once, like Luke? Or twice, like Sookie?

1	Yellow onion, cut into 4–6 thick slices
1	Duck, 3–4 lbs
	Water
1½ T	Kosher salt
1 t	Black pepper
1	Orange, quartered, plus extra for garnish
1 t	Whole cloves
2	Fresh thyme sprigs, plus extra for garnish

Chocolate Orange Sauce:

½ c	Red wine
1¼ c	Orange juice
1½ t	Molasses
1 t	Whole cloves
1 t	Black peppercorns
3 oz	Dark chocolate (60–75% cacao)

Prep oven and pan: Place oven rack in the center of oven. Preheat to 475°F. Set a roasting rack into a roasting pan. Arrange onion slices on rack. Set aside.

Prep duck: Under cool running water, rinse duck and discard any loose pieces found inside the cavity. If duck has a long neck attached, use a sharp knife to cut it at the base. Discard. Using a sharp knife or kitchen shears, remove any excess skin and/or fat from around the openings. Discard.

Boil duck: Place duck in a Dutch oven and cover the duck with water. Remove the duck and set aside. Bring the water to a boil over high heat. Add the duck back into the pot of water and boil for 10 minutes. Remove the duck from the pot and place it on a work surface.

Roast duck: Pat duck dry using paper towels. Rub the duck, inside and out, with salt and pepper. Stuff the cavity with four orange quarters, 1 teaspoon whole cloves, and 2 thyme sprigs. Place duck on top of onion slices on roasting pan rack. Place in oven. Roast for 15 minutes. Pull the pan from the oven. Carefully flip the duck. Return it to the oven and roast for an additional 15 minutes. Test the duck by inserting a meat thermometer into the thickest part of the leg. Once it reads 160°F, remove the duck from the oven. Remove duck and roasting rack from roasting pan. Tent the duck with aluminum foil.

Make the sauce: Pour the drippings from the bottom of the roasting pan into saucepan or deep frying pan, over medium-high heat. Pour in red wine. Stir to combine. Add orange juice, molasses, cloves, peppercorns, and chocolate. Stir until all ingredients combine to make a smooth sauce. Simmer 10 minutes over medium heat, stirring occasionally. Pour sauce through a strainer, into a bowl, once to remove particles. Strain sauce twice to appease Sookie.

Serve: Place duck on a platter. Garnish with additional orange quarters and sprigs of thyme, with sauce on the side.

Makes 2 servings.

BEEF JERKY

Is there no end to the things this woman can make? Yes, Sookie made Beef Jerky at home and, now, so can you.

This dish takes several hours to make—but it is very easy to prepare. Plus the ingredients make it healthier than most pre-packaged jerky sold in stores. Make a double batch of this to take on your next road trip to Harvard, or a local B&B, or Hartford on Quail Mazatlán night.

2 lb	Rib eye steak, trimmed, cut into ½-inch strips
1	Small white onion, grated
2 t	Kosher salt
1 t	Black pepper
1 t	Crushed red pepper
1 t	Smoked paprika
1 T	Worcestershire sauce
1 T	Balsamic vinegar
2 c	Water

Marinate beef: Combine all ingredients in a gallon-size bag with a zipping lock. Seal. Unseal a small section of the zipping lock. Carefully press to remove all air from bag and seal again. Refrigerate for 6 hours.

Prep oven: Place oven rack in center position. Preheat oven to 180°F.

Bake beef: Remove beef strips from marinade and arrange in a single layer on a cookie sheet. Place in oven. Bake for 4 hours. Remove pan from oven. Use paper towels to carefully remove all liquids from under each strip of beef. Turn each strip over. Return pan to oven for 4 hours. Remove from oven. If any liquids remain, pat them dry with a paper towel. Beef should be dried throughout and somewhat tough to bite into. Serve.

Makes 1 pound.

SQUAB

EMILY'S HOUSE

Squab is actually a game pigeon. It was served at Friday Night Dinner likely because it is considered a delicacy enjoyed primarily by the affluent.

Emily had her staff roast it, with a stuffing, and serve it with green beans, which is how it is prepared below. If you take a liking to its flavor and would like to experiment further, you'll find there are many delicious ways to prepare squab.

2 T	Butter, plus extra for greasing pan
2	Shallots, thinly sliced
4	Squab
2 t	Kosher salt
1 t	Black pepper

Stuffing:

2 c	French bread, cut into ½-inch cubes
2 c	Apple, peeled, cored, cut into ½-inch cubes
2 T	Minced leek (white part only)
4 T	Butter
1 T	Honey
¼ c	Red wine
¼ t	Cinnamon
¼ t	Dried thyme
1	Egg

Prep oven: Place the oven rack in the center position. Preheat oven to 375°F. Coat the bottom of a 9x14-inch baking pan with butter. Arrange a layer of shallot slices on bottom of dish. Set aside.

Toast bread: Arrange bread cubes in a single layer on a cookie sheet. Place in oven for 15 minutes. Bread will be toasted and crispy, but not browned. Remove and set aside. Increase oven temperature to 425°F.

Sauté apple: In a large frying pan, melt 4 tablespoons butter over medium heat. Add apple and leek. Sauté for 3–4 minutes. Add honey, wine, cinnamon, and thyme. Combine and sauté for 2 minutes. Remove from heat. Let stand until room temperature.

Make Stuffing: In a medium mixing bowl, mix egg until yolk and white are fully combined. Add bread cubes and apple mixture. Use hands to mix together.

Prep squab: Rinse each bird under cold water. Discard any innards. Pat dry. Stuff birds with stuffing, until bread cubes just surpass the outside edge. Use hands to rub each bird with ½ tablespoon butter. Sprinkle each bird with ½ teaspoon kosher salt and ¼ teaspoon black pepper. Place birds on top of shallot slices in baking dish. Place baking dish in oven. Bake for 15 minutes. Remove from oven. Serve.

Makes 4 squab.

LOBSTER

TOWN FAVORITE

When the Gilmore girls and their Gilmore guys head off to "The Vineyard" for Valentine's Day, Logan got the opportunity to show them what a gracious host he is. (And Luke showed what a grumpy traveler he is!)

Logan prepared lobsters for the four of them to enjoy outdoors, al fresco. He did such a good job, even Luke was won over.

Here's your chance to wow your guests. They'll be impressed. And if, at dinner, you happen to give them some diamonds, they're sure to love you forever.

	Water
½ c	Salt
4	Live lobsters, 3–4 lbs each
1 c	Butter
	Lemon wedges, for garnish

Cook lobster: Fill a Dutch oven or lobster pot about ⅔–¾ full with water. Over high heat, bring to a rolling boil. Add salt. Carefully pick up one lobster and insert into boiling water, head first. Ensure lobster is fully covered with water. Place lid on pot and let boil. Turn down heat slightly to prevent water from boiling over. Cook a 3-pound lobster for 12 minutes; a 4-pound lobster for 15 minutes. Remove lobster from water. Repeat for each lobster.

Serve or remove meat from shells: You may serve the lobsters to your guests whole, allowing them to shell their own lobster. Or, if you're using the lobster meat for another recipe, remove the meat from the shell yourself.

Melt butter: In a small saucepan, over low heat, melt butter. Once completely melted, remove from heat. Set aside.

Remove meat from claw: The majority of meat in a lobster is located in the claws and in the tail. To remove meat from claw, bend the full "arm" backward to remove it from the body. Then pull the small side of the claw down toward the arm, until it comes off. Use a nutcracker or hammer to crack the claw shell. Use a small fork to remove the meat from inside the claw.

Remove meat from tail: With one hand on the back, use the other hand to pull the tail up, until it dislodges from the body. Inside the tail you will see either green paste (male lobster) or both red and green paste (female lobster). (Allegedly both pastes are delicacies which taste great when they are spread on crackers or used in other recipes.) Under running warm-hot water, rinse the paste(s) from the tail. Then use a fork to remove the meat. Discard body and shells.

Serve: Serve lobster or lobster meat with melted butter and lemon wedges.

Makes 4 lobsters.

DEEP-FRIED TURKEY

TOWN FAVORITE

In one of the most iconic scenes of all, Jackson fries the Thanksgiving turkey, on the front lawn, while his friends chant his name. Sookie sits on the sidelines, covered in a blanket, horrified that her beautiful bird is being ruined in the deep fryer.

If you'd like to relive Jackson's Thunder Dome glory, at home, this is your chance! Just keep in mind, deep-frying a turkey is serious business. It requires you to read, understand, and abide by safety recommendations, so you can spend your time at home, enjoying turkey, rather than spending it in the E.R.

5–6 gal	Peanut oil
1	Whole turkey, 12–14 lb, fresh or *completely* thawed
2 T	Kosher salt
1 T	Black pepper

Equipment you'll need:

32-quart heavy-gauge stainless steel turkey fryer stockpot (a larger size may work)

14-inch propane-powered high pressure outdoor burner

Propane tank

ABC-rated fire extinguisher

Heavy-duty rubber safety gloves

Safety face mask

Prepare pot, burner, propane gas source, and fire extinguisher: Set up your propane source, burner, and pot outside. Place fire extinguisher within reach. Read and follow all safety recommendations carefully.

Prepare oil: Pour oil into pot, up to "max fill line" but no higher. Heat the oil to 325°F only. (If at any time, you see smoke coming from the oil, turn off the heat source immediately.)

Prep turkey: Clean turkey, removing and discarding any gizzard, neck, etc. Use a sharp knife or kitchen shears to trim any loose skin from the openings. If your turkey was frozen, it's very important that it is 100% thawed before cooking it—if any amount of water is placed in the hot oil, it can cause the oil to erupt, spilling out of the pot, possibly resulting in a fire. So use paper towels to pat the turkey dry, both outside and inside the body cavity. Mix the salt and pepper in a bowl. Use your hands to rub it all around the turkey—inside and outside. Place turkey drumsticks-down on the vertical rack.

Put turkey in oil: Once the oil has reached 325°F, with your gloves and face mask on, use the large hook to very slowly lower the turkey into the oil. It may take as long as 3 minutes to fully lower the bird. Lower it 4 inches at a time, letting the oil calm down fully before lowering another 4 inches. Once the turkey is fully submerged in the oil, the oil temperature will have lowered. Turn the flame up until the oil temperature returns to 325°F, then lower flame to maintain that temp. Cook the turkey for 3 minutes per pound. (If you have a 12-pound turkey, cook for 36 minutes.)

Test for doneness: When you pull your turkey from the oil, insert a meat thermometer into the area between the leg and the body. When it reads 160°F, the turkey is done.

Remove turkey: Turn off burner and propane gas. Remove turkey from oil. Hold over pot for 2 minutes to allow excess oil to drain into pot. Place turkey on a cutting board and let rest for 10 minutes. Carve and serve.

Makes 8–10 servings.

Cookies, Cakes

& Ice Creams

MINI LEMON BUNDT CAKES

Emily's staff serves these mini cakes for dessert the very night Emily is most concerned with size. She's so focused on the crisis caused by neighbors giving out king-size candy bars to kids for Halloween, she completely misses the joke she's masterfully set up. Not Lorelai—she's right there to serve up the sarcasm at the perfect moment, like always.

Between the fresh, moist, lemony flavor of the cake and the liqueur in the glaze, these little cakes will help you forget about any crisis in your life.

Cakes:

1½ c	Flour
½ t	Baking soda
½ t	Salt
3	Large eggs
½ c	Lemon juice, freshly squeezed
½ c	Limoncello
1 c	Granulated sugar
½ c	Olive oil

Glaze:

¼ c	Lemon juice
3 T	Mascarpone
¼ c	Limoncello
2 c	Confectioners' sugar

Prep oven and pan: Arrange oven rack in the center position. Preheat oven to 325°F. Using a mini Bundt cake pan, generously grease and flour each cup. Set aside.

Combine dry ingredients: In a medium mixing bowl, combine flour, baking soda, and salt. Set aside.

Whip egg whites: Separate eggs—put egg whites into a medium mixing bowl, put yolks into a large mixing bowl. Using a hand mixer, whip the egg whites until stiff peaks form. They should begin to look like silky, white frosting. Set aside.

Combine wet ingredients: In a measuring cup, combine lemon juice and limoncello. Set aside. To the large mixing bowl with the yolks, add the sugar. Combine using a hand mixer. Continue mixing on medium-low speed, while slowly adding olive oil, and then the lemon juice-limoncello mixture.

Finish batter: Add the dry ingredients to the wet, and mix only until combined and smooth. Using a rubber spatula or wooden spoon, fold in the egg whites and gently combine until the whites are fully incorporated into the batter.

Bake cakes: Pour the batter into each cup of the mini Bundt cake pan, filling each cup ¾ full. Place pan on the center rack in oven. Bake for 22 minutes or until a toothpick inserted into the center of a cake comes out clean. Remove from oven. Let cool for 10 minutes. Turn cakes out of pan onto cooling rack. After 10 additional minutes, cakes may be wrapped in plastic wrap to store. If they're being served right away, allow them to cool an additional 15–20 minutes.

Make glaze: Mix lemon juice and mascarpone in small mixing bowl. Mix until cheese has dissolved in liquid. Add limoncello, mix. Add confectioners' sugar. Stir until fully combined and glaze is smooth with no lumps. If there are stubborn lumps, simply strain the glaze to remove them.

Serve: This glaze is designed to be poured onto each cake as it is being served. Pour onto top of mini Bundt cake, allowing glaze to run down sides. Serve.

Makes 6–8 cakes.

Testers—Katlyn Allenson and Teri Patzwald
Eat Like a Gilmore

ROCKY ROAD COOKIES

SOOKIE'S KITCHEN

When Rory meets Dean, once she gets past her extremely awkward phase, she becomes completely smitten by him. The two begin to revolve their lives around each other. Ah . . . young love. In a gesture to show her love, Rory goes to the Independence Inn after school and asks Sookie for some of Dean's favorites: Rocky Road Cookies. Sookie happily obliges. Rory and Lane sit on a bench waiting for Dean's bus, and Rory presents Dean with the cookies. Dean's happy. Rory's happy. Lane rolls her eyes and feels sick.

The next time the sappy sweetness of your friend's new romance makes you feel sick, bake a batch of these and eat them while you list out all the benefits of being single.

2¼ c	Flour
1 t	Baking soda
½ t	Salt
1 c	Butter, room temperature
¾ c	Sugar
¾ c	Brown sugar
¾ c	Unsweetened cocoa
2	Eggs
1 t	Vanilla
¾ c	Chopped pecans
¾ c	Mini semisweet chocolate chips
1 c	Marshmallow creme (Fluff® recommended)

Prep oven and pan: Place oven rack in center of oven. Preheat to 350°F. Place parchment paper on 2 cookie sheets. Set aside.

Combine dry ingredients: In a medium mixing bowl, combine flour, baking soda, and salt. Set aside.

Combine wet ingredients: Place butter in a large mixing bowl. Add both sugars. Mix, using a hand mixer on medium-low speed. Once fully combined, add cocoa, eggs, and vanilla. Mix until combined and smooth. Using a rubber spatula, scrape down the sides of the bowl.

Make dough: Add dry ingredients to wet, in thirds, mixing after each. Combine using electric mixer, until all flour has been mixed in and dough forms. Scrape down sides of bowl. With a spatula or wooden spoon, fold in pecans and chocolate chips. Add marshmallow creme and gently fold in, so the chocolate is swirled with white from the marshmallow.

Bake cookies: Using a 1½-inch cookie scoop or a tablespoon, place rounded scoops on cookie sheet: 3 cookies wide by 4 cookies long. Bake for 10–12 minutes. Prep second cookie sheet while the first is baking. Cookies are done once they turn a bit darker brown (not too brown!). Remove from oven. Let cool for 5 minutes on cookie sheet. Move cookies to cooling racks. Cool fully before storing.

Makes approximately 30 cookies.

Note: *Mini marshmallows may be substituted for marshmallow creme. Do not add them to the batter. Bake the cookies without marshmallows. As the baked cookies come out of the oven, insert 4–5 marshmallows into each cookie. Let them cool for 10 minutes, then serve.*

Tester—Kendall Gibson

HOMEMADE TWINKIES

EMILY'S HOUSE

Emily instructed her staff make these as a special surprise for Rory, the night Rory brought Dean over for dinner. Lorelai and Rory were both excited at the idea of trying homemade Twinkies®, especially when Emily called to the maid to bring them out to the table. But Richard's interrogation of Dean spoiled the fun. Rory got angry and left before she got to taste a single bite. It was a disappointment for all of us.

Here's our chance to relive that moment: a do-over. For goodness sake, this time, hang around long enough to try a homemade Twinkie!

Cakes:

1 c	Flour
2 t	Baking powder
¼ t	Salt
4	Eggs
½ t	Cream of tartar
¾ c	Whole milk
½ c	Butter, melted
1½ c	Sugar
2 t	Vanilla

Filling:

2	Egg whites
¼ t	Cream of tartar
1 c	Marshmallow creme (Fluff recommended)

Prep oven and pan: Position oven rack so it is one notch higher than the center (top third of oven). Preheat to 350°F. Generously grease and flour specialty cake pan. Set aside.

Combine dry ingredients: In a medium bowl, combine flour, baking powder, and salt. Set aside.

Whip up egg whites: Separate 4 eggs—place whites in medium mixing bowl; place yolks in large mixing bowl. Add ½ teaspoon cream of tartar to whites. Using a hand mixer, beat egg whites, gradually increasing speed, until stiff peaks form. Once whites look like silky, white frosting, they're ready. Set aside.

Combine milk and butter: In a glass measuring cup, measure milk. Add melted butter and mix. Set aside.

Make batter: Using a hand mixer, beat egg yolks until smooth. Add sugar and vanilla. Mix. Add dry ingredients and mix until flour has been fully incorporated into batter. Pour in milk-butter combination and mix only until combined. Using a spatula or wooden spoon, fold in egg whites and gently mix until fully blended.

Bake cakes: In the baking pan, pour batter into each cup until it is nearly full. Repeat for each cup. Place in oven and bake for 22–25 minutes. Look for a golden brown ring around each cake. Insert a toothpick into one of the center cakes; when it comes out clean, remove cakes from oven. Let cool for 10 minutes. Turn cakes out onto cooling rack—allow to cool completely before piping in the filling.

Make filling: Place 2 egg whites and ¼ teaspoon cream of tartar in a large mixing bowl. Once again, use a hand mixer to beat egg whites, gradually increasing speed, until stiff peaks form. Once whites look like silky, white frosting, they are ready. Add marshmallow creme. Mix until fully combined. This is your filling.

Pipe filling into cakes: Using a piping bag—either the one that came with the cake pan or a regular frosting bag with a sharp tip—add the filling to the bag. Then poke the tip into the bottom of each cake 3 times—once in the middle, then once on each side. Pipe about ⅔ teaspoon of filling into each hole—so each cake will have about 2 teaspoons of filling, total.

Serve.

Makes 20 cakes.

Testers—Revs. Krystal and John Leedy

Eat Like a Gilmore

BLUEBERRY SHORTCAKE

CONTRIBUTED BY HEATHER BURSON

SOOKIE'S KITCHEN

Gilmore Girls gave us some great lessons on making the most with what you have. This dessert is a prime example. When Sookie is left in the lurch, unable to get strawberries to make strawberry shortcake, she thinks up a creative solution: Blueberry Shortcake!

The next time you think up an ingenious solution to a problem, make this for yourself to celebrate! Then take the rest of it to work or a friend's gathering. It's so delicious, no one's going to care that it's used.

Blueberry Filling:

6 c	**Fresh blueberries, divided**
1	**Lemon, zested, and juiced to equal ¼ cup liquid**
½ c	**Sugar**
⅓ c + 1 t	**Cold water, divided**
¼ t	**Ground ginger**
2 t	**Cornstarch**

Make Blueberry Filling:

- Rinse blueberries and drain thoroughly.

- In a medium saucepan, place 3 cups berries, lemon zest, lemon juice, sugar, ⅓ cup water, and the ground ginger.

- Bring pan to a simmer, until sugar is dissolved, berries are plump, and color starts to seep into the water.

- In a small cup, mix 2 teaspoons cornstarch with 1 teaspoon cold water until smooth. Pour cornstarch mixture into simmering blueberries and stir well.

- Continue stirring gently until mixture begins to bubble and thicken.

- Remove pan from heat and allow to cool completely. Once cooled, stir in remaining 3 cups of blueberries. Transfer berry filling to bowl, cover with plastic wrap, and refrigerate overnight. Mixture will continue to thicken as it chills.

Lemon Curd:

3	Large lemons, zested, and juiced to equal ¾ cup liquid
1½ c	Superfine sugar
4	Large eggs
1	Large egg yolk
½ c	Cubed unsalted butter

Shortcakes:

2 c	Flour
1 T	Baking powder
½ t	Baking soda
¼ t	Salt
¼ t	Ground ginger
¼ t	Ground cinnamon
⅓ c	Sugar
¼ c	Unsalted butter, cold
2 T	Shortening, cold
¾ c	Heavy cream
1 t	Vanilla
1	Large lemon, zested (TIP: reserve juice for lemon curd or blueberry filling)
2	Large eggs, divided
1 t	Water
	Coarse sugar, for sprinkling

Make Lemon Curd:

- In a medium saucepan, whisk together lemon zest, lemon juice, sugar, eggs, and egg yolk until sugar is thoroughly dissolved and eggs are fully incorporated.

- Place saucepan on medium heat and add cubed butter.

- Stir constantly until butter has melted, being careful to scrape down the sides and bottom of the pan.

- Keep stirring until mixture is thick and similar in consistency to warm pudding. The curd is finished when it coats the back of a spoon and leaves a trail when a spoon is dragged through the pan.

- Transfer Lemon Curd to bowl. Cover mixture with plastic wrap—the plastic wrap should rest directly on the curd to prevent a "skin" from forming.

- Allow to cool completely. For best results, refrigerate overnight.

Make Shortcakes:

- Preheat oven to 400°F. Line baking sheets with parchment paper.

- In a large bowl, sift together flour, baking powder, baking soda, salt, ginger, cinnamon, and sugar.

- Add in cubed butter and shortening, using a pastry cutter, until mixture resembles pea-sized gravel.

- Gently pour in heavy cream, vanilla, lemon zest, and 1 egg. Mix gently with wooden spoon until just barely combined. DO NOT OVER-MIX.

- Turn dough out onto floured surface. Knead until dough comes together in a smooth form. Flatten into disc.

- Using a biscuit cutter, cut out shortcakes and place on lined baking sheets.

- In a small bowl, whisk remaining egg and 1 teaspoon water until well blended to make an egg wash.

- Using a pastry brush, top each shortcake with egg wash and sprinkle with coarse sugar.

- Bake for 15–18 minutes, or until golden.

- Transfer cakes to cooling racks and allow to cool completely.

Tester—Heather Burson

Whipped Cream:

2	Whole Madagascar bourbon vanilla beans
2 c	Heavy cream
½ c	Superfine sugar
¼ c	Sour cream

Make Whipped Cream:

- Chill large mixing bowl and beaters or whisk attachment in freezer for 30 minutes.

- Slice vanilla beans lengthwise and scrape out seeds. Add seeds to chilled bowl along with heavy cream and sugar. With mixer set on medium speed, beat until stiff peaks form.

- Add sour cream to bowl and beat on high until stiff peaks form again.

- Cover bowl with plastic wrap and chill until ready to assemble dessert.

Fresh mint, for garnish

Dessert assembly:

- Slice each shortcake in half and arrange bottoms on dessert plates.

- Begin by layering shortcake bottoms with fresh lemon curd.

- Add a generous scoop of blueberry filling on top of lemon curd.

- Follow with a spoonful of whipped cream on top of the blueberries.

- Place top half of shortcake back on top of the layered filling.

- Finish with additional dollop of whipped cream and a sprig of fresh mint.

- Serve immediately.

- Makes 6–8 shortcakes.

CARAMEL MARSHMALLOW
CHOCOLATE CHUNK COOKIES

SOOKIE'S KITCHEN

To launch the Dragonfly Inn, Lorelai, Sookie, and Michel organized a "preview tour" which they held the day before the inn officially opened to the public. Members of the travel industry were on hand for the tour, with a charming and witty version of Michel as their guide. Sookie knew this was an important chance to grab their attention with her food. She needed something unique, something to "wow" the visitors. She chose these.

These cookies definitely smell, look, and taste like fancy "preview tour" fare. Make these when you want to leave a positive, lasting, "tell your friends" kind of impression.

Cookies:

2¼ c	Flour
1 t	Baking soda
½ t	Cream of tartar
1 t	Kosher salt
14	Large vegan marshmallows
16 oz	Semisweet chocolate chunks or bar
1 c	Butter, room temperature
½ c	Granulated sugar
½ c	Light brown sugar, packed
1 T	Molasses
2	Large eggs, room temperature
1 t	Vanilla

Caramel Topping:

1 c	Heavy whipping cream, room temperature
4 T	Butter
2 t	Vanilla
2 T	Light corn syrup
2 c	Granulated sugar
½ c	Water

For Cookies:

Prep oven and trays: Ensure oven rack is placed in the center of oven. Preheat oven to 350°F. Line cookie sheet(s) with parchment paper.

Combine dry ingredients: In a medium-sized mixing bowl, combine flour, baking soda, cream of tartar, and salt. Set aside.

Prepare add-ins: Cut marshmallows in half, across the narrow middle. Break chocolate chunks/bar into small pieces—until each is roughly ½x½-inch square.

Mix cookie dough: In a large mixing bowl, combine butter, both sugars, and molasses. Begin mixing using a hand mixer on low setting, increasing to medium speed. Mix until fully combined and smooth. Scrape down sides of the bowl with a rubber spatula. Add eggs and vanilla. Mix on medium speed until fully combined. Add in the dry ingredients one third at a time—begin on medium speed, increasing to high speed— until all ingredients are fully combined. Dough will form and pull away from the sides of the bowl.

Form and bake cookies: Using a 1½-inch scoop or a tablespoon, scoop dough into 1½-inch balls. Round each ball by hand-rolling it. Tear the ball into two halves. Sandwich a marshmallow piece between the two halves, then roll the dough back into a ball, fully covering the marshmallow. Place the ball on cookie sheet, and flatten slightly with palm of hand. Evenly space 12 cookies on each sheet and bake for 10–12 minutes. Remove from oven when cookies are medium golden brown.

Add-in chocolate chunks: Immediately insert 3–5 pieces of chocolate, strategically spaced, into the top of each cookie. Then move cookies from cookie sheet to a wire rack to cool.

(Be careful not to bump the chocolate pieces once they're inserted—as the chocolate will be very soft/melty. Once the cookies cool, the chocolate will harden again, and take its original shape.) While cookies are cooling, prepare the Caramel Topping.

For Caramel Topping:

Prepare add-ins: In separate dishes, measure the heavy cream, butter, and vanilla.

Heat the syrup, sugar, and water: In a large saucepan or Dutch oven, combine the corn syrup, sugar, and water. Stir until combined and begin heating. Over high heat, bring to a boil. Using a candy thermometer, allow the mixture to boil, without stirring, until the temperature reaches "Hard Ball" stage (250°–265°F).

Create caramel: Both the mixture and pan will be extremely hot. Very carefully, standing back from the stove a bit, using a heat resistant rubber spatula, stir in the heavy cream until fully blended. Then do the same with the butter. Again, heat mixture without stirring, until it reaches "Soft Ball" stage (235°–240°F). Remove from heat. Very carefully, standing slightly away from the stove, stir in vanilla. Continue stirring until vanilla is fully blended and caramel has reduced in volume. This is your caramel topping!

Add caramel to cookies: Using a teaspoon, directly from the pan, drizzle 1 teaspoon of caramel topping across each cookie, back and forth in horizontal lines. Serve.

Let cookies cool completely before storing.

Makes 2 dozen cookies.

MUFFIN BOTTOM & PUDDING PIE

CONTRIBUTED BY SHEHZEEN AHMED & MEHREEN AHMED

Ever since watching the episode in Season 7 when Sookie mentions she made this pie, we have wondered just how she created it.

For this project, we discussed many different theories about how to use the infamous muffin bottoms. We collected all of our ideas and headed into the kitchen to experiment with each one.

After much testing, this recipe is the clear winner. Enjoy!

Crust:

6 T	Butter, melted
1½ c	Crushed graham crackers (about one package from the box)
¼ c	Sugar

Filling:

3 c	Vanilla Pudding, from page 231, or 5.1-oz box of instant pudding mix
16 oz	Whipped topping (Cool Whip©, recommended)
6	Muffin bottoms, large
1 can	Whipped cream

Make crust: In a medium bowl, mix melted butter with crushed graham crackers and sugar. When mixture looks like wet sand, press it into the bottom and sides of a standard 8–inch pie pan.

Make filling: In a medium bowl, fold pudding into whipped topping. Combine until fully blended.

Assemble pie: With a sharp knife, slice muffin bottoms in half, horizontally, so you have two circles from each muffin bottom. Place six slices on graham cracker crust to create a muffin bottom layer. Using half of the whipped topping mix, layer it over the muffin bottom layer, filling in the spaces between the muffin bottoms. Place remaining six slices of muffin bottoms on top of whipped topping layer. Add remaining whipped topping to cover muffin bottoms.

Top with whipped cream: Cover the top in a decorative layer of whipped cream. Add any desired garnish. Garnish can depend on the muffins being used (e.g., for double chocolate chip muffins, use chocolate shavings; for lemon poppy seed, use fresh berries, etc.).

Chill pie and serve: Chill for at least 1 hour; can be stored overnight in the fridge. Serve.

Makes 8 servings.

OATMEAL COOKIES

When Lorelai announces to Rory and Sookie that the acceptance letter to Chilton arrived, excited squealing ensued. Each of them reacted in their own special way. Lorelai immediately jumped on the opportunity to buy new clothes, presenting Rory with her new school uniform. Rory was immediately worried—thinking that she got in because her mother got naked with the headmaster. And Sookie, of course, baked. This is what she made: Oatmeal Cookies.

These aren't really the most "celebratory" cookies—maybe Sookie intuitively knew what a hard time Rory would have once she got to Chilton.

If you're taking these to church, they're perfect. (Protestants will love them!) But if you're serving them at a celebration, top them with whipped cream and sprinkles, or sandwich some ice cream between them—transform them into something FUN!

2 c	Flour
1 t	Baking soda
1 t	Salt
1 t	Cinnamon
½ t	Ground cloves
½ t	Ground nutmeg
½ t	Ground allspice
1 c	Butter, soft
1½ c	Brown sugar
2	Eggs
⅓ c	Molasses
1 T	Vanilla
3 c	Old-fashioned oats
	Chocolate chips, optional
	Raisins, optional

Prep oven and pans: Place oven racks in center of oven. Preheat oven to 375°F. Cover the bottom of 2 cookie sheets with parchment paper. Set aside.

Mix dry ingredients: In a medium bowl, combine flour, baking soda, salt, cinnamon, cloves, nutmeg, and allspice. Set aside.

Mix wet ingredients: In a large mixing bowl, add butter and sugar. Use a mixer on medium speed to combine. Add eggs. Mix to combine. Add molasses and vanilla. Mix to combine. Add dry ingredients in thirds, mixing to combine each time. Use a spatula to scrape down the sides of the bowl. Fold in oats (and chocolate chips or raisins, if desired).

Bake cookies: Using a 1½-inch cookie scoop or a rounded tablespoon, drop 15 evenly spaced cookies on each tray. Place in oven. Bake for 10 minutes. Remove. Let cool on trays for 5 minutes. Remove cookies and place them on cooling rack(s) for 10 minutes. Serve.

Makes 30 cookies.

DESSERT SUSHI

Over the years of the series, whenever Rory suffered a disappointment or setback, Lorelai supported her, consoled her, and cheered her back up. When Rory got a "D" on a paper, Lorelai sat up all night studying with her. When Rory had her heart broken by Dean, Lorelai was there, coaxing her to wallow.

So when Rory's Asia trip gets canceled unexpectedly, it's the most natural thing for Lorelai to attempt to console her by creating Asia in their house. Warning: The candy combinations in these dessert sushi rolls are not natural; it's what makes them perfectly Lorelai.

6 rolls	Fruit by the Foot®, any flavor (preferably different colors)
	Marshmallow creme (Fluff recommended)
27	Red licorice twists
54	Tootsie Rolls®
27	Butterfinger® Bites
27	Jujubes®
54	Chocolate chips
27	Junior Mints®

Prep rolls: Unravel 6 Fruit by the Foot rolls, and lay them out on a work surface. Cut each one into nine 4-inch lengths. Use a spatula to spread a thin layer of marshmallow creme on one half of each piece (2 inches of the piece will have marshmallow, 2 inches will be empty).

Make roll #1: On 27 of the 4-inch pieces, sideways across the marshmallow, place 3 pieces of licorice, cut to size, and 2 Tootsie Rolls. Roll each one, beginning at the marshmallow side. Trim any excess licorice. Place rolls on a plate. Set aside.

Make roll #2: On the remaining 27 4-inch pieces, place 1 Butterfinger Bite, 1 Jujube, 2 chocolate chips, and 1 Junior Mint. Roll each one, beginning at the marshmallow side. Place rolls on a plate.

Serve.

Makes 27 pieces of each, 54 total.

CHOCOLATE CHOCOLATE CHOCOLATE ICE CREAM

TOWN FAVORITE

Taylor was inspired when he had the thought to open an old-fashioned soda and candy shop(pe) in town. Even his manipulative dealings as Town Selectman can't keep people away from the candy, sodas, hot chocolate, and ice cream he serves up in the shop.

After seeing Rory's reaction when she tried Taylor's ice cream, I really wanted this version to live up to the name. To give depth to the chocolate flavor, I blended three different chocolates. The result is a rich, velvety treat, just like the one on the show. Fair warning—this is an ice cream for the serious chocoholic.

	Water
½ c	Dark chocolate, 70% cacao or higher
½ c	Milk chocolate chips
½ c	White chocolate
⅔ c	Sweetened condensed milk
2¼ c	Whole milk
½ c	Coffee, brewed strongly
½ c	Mini chocolate chips, optional

Melt chocolate: Fill a large saucepan with 1–2 inches of water. Heat over medium heat. Place a smaller saucepan inside (to mimic a double boiler). Add dark chocolate, then milk chocolate, then white chocolate to the smaller saucepan. Use a spatula to stir chocolate every few minutes.

Mix in milks and coffee: Add sweetened condensed milk to chocolates. Mix thoroughly. Add whole milk and coffee. Mix thoroughly. Once a thick, smooth, chocolate sauce forms, remove from heat. Transfer sauce to a bowl and refrigerate for 2 hours.

Make ice cream: Remove chocolate sauce from refrigerator. Turn on ice cream maker. Pour chocolate sauce into maker and churn into ice cream, for approximately 20 minutes. Times will vary based on several factors. Watch for a thick, frosting-like consistency. (If you're adding chocolate chips, add them now, and then churn until fully combined.) Transfer ice cream to a plastic container. Cover with a tight-fitting lid, and freeze for 6 hours.

Serve.

Makes 4–6 servings.

APPLE TARTS

When Lorelai gets herself uninvited from Emily and Richard's Christmas Party, we learn that one of her primary reasons for attending each year (possibly *the* reason for attending) is the opportunity to eat Apple Tarts. She loves them so well, she's made up songs about them.

If you like a good caramel apple, then you'll love these, like Lorelai. Try them at home and see what all the songwriting is about.

Butter or shortening, for preparing pan

Flour, for preparing pan and rolling crust

Crust:

1½ c	Flour
1 t	Baking powder
¼ c	Sugar
¼ t	Salt
10 T	Butter
2	Egg yolks
1 T	Sour cream
½ t	Vanilla

Filling:

8 T	Butter
8 T	Sugar
8 T	Brown sugar
6	Apples (Fuji recommended), peeled, sliced thinly
	Cinnamon

Prep oven and pan: Place oven rack in center position. Preheat oven to 400°F. Grease and flour a standard or mini muffin pan or a tart pan. Set aside.

Make crust: In a medium mixing bowl, combine flour, baking powder, sugar, and salt. Cut in butter using a pastry blender (alternatively, cut butter into small cubes ahead of time, then cut into flour mixture using two butter knives). In a mixing cup or small bowl, beat egg yolks. Add sour cream and vanilla and mix. Pour into dry ingredients and mix with a fork until dough forms.

Form crust: Flour a work surface and rolling pin. Roll dough into a flat, round shape, about ¼-inch thick.

If you're making individual tarts: Use a glass that is ½–1-inch wider than the cups in the pan you're using to cut the dough into circles. Press each circle into one of the pan's cups. Press the dough into the corners of the cup. The dough should come up ¼–½ inch on the sides. Use a fork to prick the bottom of each tart 3–4 times, to keep the dough from rising too much as it bakes.

If you're making one large tart: press the dough into the tart pan, taking care to press dough into the edge of the pan, so the bottom is flat all the way to the edges. The dough should extend up the sides of the pan about ½–1 inch. Use a fork to prick the bottom 10–12 times, to prevent the dough from rising too much as it bakes.

Bake crust: Place crust in oven and bake for 15 minutes. Remove from oven and set aside.

Make filling: In a large saucepan, over medium heat, melt butter. Add both sugars, and stir. Add apples and stir to combine. Cook apple mixture for 10 minutes, until apple pieces are tender and surrounded by a gooey light brown syrup. Remove from heat.

Assemble and bake tarts: Arrange apple pieces in each tart. Pour syrup over each tart until it reaches ¾ of the way up the side of the crust. Bake tarts for 8 minutes. Remove from oven. Let cool for 10 minutes. Remove tarts from pan. Lightly sprinkle each one with cinnamon. Serve.

Makes 6–8 individual tarts or 1 (10-inch) tart.

PIZZELLES

SOOKIE'S KITCHEN

Some of the most inspiring *Gilmore Girls* episodes take place when Lorelai and Sookie (and Michel) become entrepreneurs. Viewers get to sit in the front row, watching while they progress from dreaming about their own inn, to losing their jobs, to finding and negotiating the purchase of the Dragonfly Estate, through construction and design, money troubles, wooing Michel away from Celine Dion, writing their first reservation on a gum wrapper, the Canadian stove fiasco, Lorelai's overgrown hair, sleeping in the zucchini patch, and finally, the grand opening!

This recipe comes from that era. When Sookie was home with newborn Davey, she had Tobin care for the baby (!!!) while she experimented in the kitchen. This was one of her experiments: Pizzelles.

Anise is used here because it is the traditional Italian flavor of Pizzelles. But you can experiment with any flavor you like; simply swap out the anise for the flavor of your choice—vanilla, almond, orange, lemon. (If you try orange or lemon, add ½ teaspoon of zest to the batter.) Try each one—then invite Lorelai and Michel over for a tasting.

1¾ c	**Flour**
2 t	**Baking powder**
½ c	**Butter, room temperature**
¾ c	**Sugar**
3	**Eggs**
1 t	**Anise extract**
	Confectioners' sugar, for dusting

Combine dry ingredients: In a small bowl, mix flour and baking powder. Set aside.

Combine wet ingredients: In a small mixing bowl, with an electric mixer, cream butter and sugar together. Add eggs. Mix until fully combined. Add anise extract. Mix just enough to blend into batter.

Finish batter: Mix dry ingredients into wet, using electric mixer.

Make Pizzelles: Heat pizzelle maker. Once it's ready, spoon a rounded teaspoon of batter onto the center of each mold. Close lid. Cook for 30 seconds, exactly. Quickly remove pizzelles and place them on a flat surface. (If you're making them into cannoli shells or waffle cones, mold the pizzelles into the desired shape right as you pull them from the mold.) Let them cool for 5 minutes. Repeat until all of the batter has been used. Dust with confectioners' sugar. Serve.

Makes 25–30 pizzelles.

DOUBLE CHOCOLATE BROWNIES

Over the years, Lorelai asked Luke for countless favors, from fixing windows to borrowing thirty thousand dollars. Some favors, she didn't even need to ask for—he just did them without any provocation, like sharpening the blades on her ice skates, shoveling her driveway, and building her a chuppah. The entire foundation of their relationship was built on Luke doing things for Lorelai.

Considering everything he'd done for her, the first time Luke asked Lorelai for a favor—her "yes, sure!" answer should have been a given. Buuuut the favor involved Rory spending time with Jess, to tutor him. So for Luke to get a "yes," he knew he needed to sweeten the deal. He did, with these brownies.

With twice as much cocoa as regular brownies, these are sure to get a "yes" out of anyone.

	Butter or shortening, for preparing pan
½ c	Flour, plus extra for preparing pan
1 c	Unsweetened cocoa
½ t	Baking soda
½ t	Salt
2	Eggs
1 c	Sugar
1 t	Vanilla
½ c	Melted butter
¼ c	Whole milk

Prep oven and pans: Place oven rack in center of oven. Preheat oven to 350°F. Grease and flour an 8x8-inch baking pan. Set aside.

Mix dry ingredients: In a medium bowl, mix flour, cocoa, baking soda, and salt. Set aside.

Mix wet ingredients: In a medium mixing bowl, mix eggs until yolks and whites are fully combined. Mix in sugar and vanilla. Add melted butter. Stir to combine.

Make batter: Add dry ingredients to wet ingredients, mixing just enough to combine. Add milk and mix to combine. Pour batter into prepared baking pan.

Bake brownies: Place pan in oven. Bake for 25 minutes. Test for doneness by inserting a toothpick into the center. When toothpick comes out clean, remove pan from oven. Let cool for 5 minutes. Gently turn pan over, until brownie pops out. Cool whole brownie on cooling rack for 10 minutes. Cut and serve.

Makes 16 brownies.

BAKED ALASKA

SOOKIE'S KITCHEN

When Sookie is at work, she cooks. When she gets home, she cooks. When she's in love, she cooks. When she's happy, she cooks. When she's stricken with a case of ennui—she sits with her head in her hands and stares at the floor. But once the ennui is lifted? That's right. She cooks.

Sookie whipped up this dish when she was procrastinating. Rather than pick up the phone and plan a date with Jackson, Sookie decided to experiment with a new type of Baked Alaska for dessert.

This isn't in the shape of Alaska, but you'll forget all about that idea after the first bite.

1 pt	Dulce de leche ice cream, softened
1 pt	Vanilla ice cream, softened
1 pt	Coffee ice cream, softened
1 batch	Double Chocolate Brownies, uncut (see page 227)

Meringue:

¾ c	Egg whites (about 5–6 eggs' worth)
2¼ c	Sugar
¾ c	Water

Mold ice cream: In a 7-inch metal or glass bowl, use a spatula to spread the dulce de leche ice cream into a flat layer on the bottom of the bowl. Add a second layer by spreading vanilla ice cream. Add third layer by spreading coffee ice cream. Cover with plastic wrap. Freeze on a level surface for 1 hour.

Add crust: Remove bowl from freezer. Turn 8x8-inch brownie square upside down onto bowl, ensuring it's centered with the bowl. Press down to push brownie into bowl (the corners of the brownie will crumble off). Cover with plastic wrap. Freeze on a level surface for 2 hours.

Beat egg whites: In a medium mixing bowl, with a mixer, beat the egg whites. Start on medium low speed and work your way up to full speed. Continue beating until stiff, shiny, white peaks form. Set aside.

Make syrup: In a saucepan, over medium-high heat, combine sugar and water. Insert a candy thermometer. Stir sugar-water until temperature reaches 235°–240°F (no hotter!). Remove syrup from heat.

Make meringue: Turn on mixer. Slowly drizzle syrup into egg whites, taking care to mix the syrup into the whites the second it hits the bowl. (Otherwise, the heat of the syrup will cook the egg whites, and that's not festive.) Continue to mix until all syrup has been incorporated.

Make Baked Alaska: Remove bowl from freezer. Turn it upside down onto a serving plate. When it pops out, you will have a brownie foundation, topped by three layers of ice cream. Use a spatula to cover the ice cream and brownie with a layer of meringue. Using a kitchen torch (Carefully! Remember the Chilton bake sale!), lightly torch the outside of the meringue. Tips and ridges should be brown, but not burnt. Serve.

Makes 1 (8-inch) Baked Alaska.

PUDDING

This isn't Mrs. Kim's multi-grain soy pudding. No way. This is crafted after the pudding Emily served Lorelai and Rory in crystal bowls. It's a pudding-lover's pudding. Even though it's made from scratch, this recipe is not much more difficult than making a boxed mix—it's possibly more foolproof! After a few bites of this stuff, you'll understand why Lorelai worships Pudding!

1 T	Butter
1 T	Vanilla
2 c	Whole milk, cold
3 T	Cornstarch
3	Egg yolks
¾ c	Sugar
¼ t	Kosher salt

For Lemon Pudding: **Replace vanilla with ½ cup fresh lemon juice**

For Chocolate Pudding: **With the vanilla, add ½ cup chocolate fudge topping**

For Tapioca Pudding: **Add ¼ cup instant tapioca to pan before heating**

Prepare butter and vanilla: Measure and set out both butter and vanilla, so you can access them in a hurry.

Combine milk and cornstarch: Measure milk, and while it's still in the measuring cup, add cornstarch and gently whisk until the two are fully combined.

Make pudding: In a medium saucepan, combine egg yolks, sugar, and salt. Do not stir. Pour in milk-cornstarch mixture. Whisk together until smooth. Turn on heat to medium-high setting. Continue stirring while pudding heats. It will thicken right before it boils. So watch for bubbles around the edges —when they appear, it indicates the pudding is about to boil. Turn off heat. Stir in butter and vanilla.

Chill pudding: Pour pudding into a bowl or container. Place a layer of plastic wrap directly on the pudding. Refrigerate for 90 minutes. Serve.

CAKERY

-Mandi

IF YOU can make a PB&J, you can stack a cake. In the cake world, we use all kinds of jargon like "torting" and "damming" when we talk about stacking and filling cakes. Don't be intimidated by terminology. It's just like making a sandwich . . . a moist, delicious sandwich.

LEVEL: There is nothing better than a cake that bakes perfectly with a golden dome reaching up out of its pan. But domes are hard to stack. Because physics. So level, flat-top cake layers are much better for stacking. The two easiest ways to level cake layers is with a cake leveler (yay for buying cake gear!) or by pressing. To press your cake, cover the top of your still-hot cake layer with a clean (does that need to be said?) dish towel. Gently press the towel onto the dome of the cake. Then, flip your cake onto the dish towel on your counter to cool. Cover it up while it cools so it won't get all dry.

TORTE: You can use just about anything as a filling between cake layers. Jam, jelly, cream, pie filling, pudding, fresh fruit, marshmallow creme—the sky's the limit! Stacking cake layers with something good in between them is called "torting." Sounds fancy, right?

DAM: If you want to use a loose or runnier filling, you can dam your cake layers. This just means you squirt a ring of something thick—like the buttercream you're going to use to ice your cake—around the outer edge of the bottom cake layer before you add the filling in the middle. Kinda like a really lame, wide bull's-eye. The icing keeps the soft filling from squirting out the sides of the cake when you stack on your cake layers. It acts as a dam for the filling. Get it?

CRUMB COAT: Once you have your nice, flat layers stacked and torted, add a thin layer of your icing to the outside of the cake. They call it a crumb coat because, when you're icing a cake, your spatula tends to pick up some crumbs, which can make your icing look spotty. If you apply a thin crumb coat first and then chill the cake in the fridge for a few minutes, when you ice it, the crumbs will be trapped safely beneath the surface everyone sees in the end. It's like primer. Cake primer.

LAYERS vs TIERS: When you cut yourself a piece of cake, you'll see stripes of alternating cake and filling. Those cake stripes are your cake layers. Most of my party cakes have three layers. When you look at a cake (before it's cut) and see a little cake stacked on top of a larger cake, those are tiers. Wedding cakes used to be about the only tiered cakes in town, but these days, any event can have a cake with more than one tier. It is very important—*very* important—that you use proper structure when you stack tiers. Dowels, pillars, bubble tea straws, stainless steel support systems . . . there are a lot of ways to stack tiers. Do not stack tiers without support. Just . . . no.

DECORATING THE CAKE: In the weeks that will pass between me writing this paragraph and this book being published, at least three new cake techniques and trends will sweep through the cake world. American buttercream, Swiss meringue buttercream, Italian meringue buttercream, ganache, royal icing, fondant, modeling chocolate . . . there are so many ways to cover a cake. And each cake covering has its own options for decorating techniques. There is always something new and fun to learn. Check out online cake schools or your local cake decorating instructors to find out how to use all the different sugar media.

DARK CHOCOLATE S'MORES WEDDING CAKE

SOOKIE'S KITCHEN

After Sookie created the formal, traditional, tiered white cake for Lorelai's wedding to Max (RIP Clyde), she must have realized that style wasn't really suited to Lorelai's personality (as it turned out, neither was Max). So once Lorelai got engaged to Luke, Sookie dreamed up a truly inspired, Lorelai-esque cake: a s'mores wedding cake. Sadly, Luke and Lorelai's wedding never took place either. So no one got to try the cake! Until now.

	Butter or shortening, for preparing pan(s)
	Flour, for preparing pan(s)
2 c	Graham cracker crumbs
½ c	Ground pecans (walnuts may be substituted)
¾ c	Flour
2 t	Baking powder
¼ t	Salt
3	Eggs, separated
¾ c	Butter, room temperature
¾ c	Sugar
½ c	Brown sugar
1 t	Vanilla
1 c	Whole milk, room temperature
	Chocolate Fudge Icing (see page 239) or your favorite homemade chocolate ganache
	Marshmallow creme (Fluff recommended)

Prep oven and pans: Preheat oven to 350°F. Place two oven racks in the center of the oven, one rung apart from each other. Grease and flour three 8-inch round cake pans.

Combine dry ingredients: Combine graham cracker crumbs, ground nuts, flour, baking powder, and salt in a bowl and set aside.

Whip egg whites: In a medium mixing bowl, using a hand mixer, whip the whites at high speed until stiff peaks form. Set aside.

Combine wet ingredients: In a large mixing bowl, using a hand mixer on medium speed, cream together butter and both sugars until fluffy. Switch mixer speed to low and add vanilla. Add egg yolks.

Make batter: Alternate adding dry ingredients and milk into wet ingredients: add one third dry ingredients, mix until combined, add one third of the milk, mix until combined, repeat, scraping down sides of the bowl with a spatula in between rounds. Then use a wooden spoon or spatula to fold in egg whites just until they're combined.

Bake cakes: Divide batter evenly among your cake pans. Arrange pans in oven with at least 3 inches between them, and at least 3 inches from the sides of the oven. Bake at 350°F for 20–25 minutes. To check doneness, lightly press on the top of the cake. When the top springs back, the cake is done.

Cool and wrap cakes: Allow to cool for 10–15 minutes. While cakes are still warm, wrap them in plastic wrap. This will help retain moisture. Allow cakes to cool completely before decorating.

(Continued on next page)

Assemble the cake: Wait until the cake layers have completely cooled. Level one of your layers and place it on your cake board. Put some fudge icing or dark chocolate ganache in a piping bag or zip-locking bag. Snip off the bag's tip or corner and squeeze a thick layer of icing on the cake layer. Draw the biggest circle of icing you can on the top of the cake—aim for the edge. Fill the inside of your icing ring with marshmallow creme. Stack another leveled layer of cake on top and repeat the icing ring and marshmallow creme steps on the top of this one. Add your final layer of leveled cake to the top.

Ice and decorate the outside of the cake: Ice the cake with dark chocolate ganache or fudge icing. Decorate with marshmallows and/or edible gold leaf. If you're feeling frisky, you can brown your marshmallow decorations with a small kitchen blowtorch. Bonus points if you dress like a reboot Ghostbuster while you use the blowtorch.

Irene's Decorating Tips:

- Use chocolate fondant to recreate the band on the top of the s'mores cake; then paint it with edible gold dust.

- Soften the fondant by kneading it, but don't over-work it.

- To prevent sticking, lightly coat the work surface and hands with a thin layer of shortening.

- Gold dust (also called gold highlighter) can be found online.

- Place the fondant band onto the cake before painting it with the gold dust.

- Edible gold paint is available online or at cake supply stores. You can make your own using gold petal dust, also called edible gold highlighter.

- To make edible gold paint: Put a little bit of gold dust (⅛ teaspoon) in a small container (like a tiny sushi/soy sauce plate). Add a few drops of vodka or lemon extract. Apply it to the fondant with a clean paintbrush reserved only for this purpose.

- Cut the marshmallows with scissors.

- Keep cornstarch handy when working with the sticky marshmallows.

DARK CHOCOLATE ESPRESSO CAKE

SOOKIE'S KITCHEN

Should you find yourself in a situation where you need to carve a cake into the shape of . . . say . . . a golf ball or a graduation tassel hat, use pound cake—it's more sturdy. All of my pound cake recipes are based off the most popular of all pound cakes: The Elvis. It is based on the recipe Elvis Presley used, himself, to make pound cake (you can't go wrong with heavy whipping cream and seven eggs—that's a solid life lesson right there).

This *Gilmore* pound cake gives The Elvis a little twist.

Butter or shortening, for preparing pan(s)

Flour, for preparing pan(s)

Cake:

3 c	Cake flour
¾ c	Cocoa
1 c	Butter, room temperature
3 c	Sugar
7	Large eggs, room temperature
1 t	Vanilla
1 t	Salt
1 c	Heavy cream
2 T	Espresso powder

Chocolate Fudge Icing:

2 c	Chocolate-covered espresso beans
½ c	Butter
½–¾ c	Unsweetened cocoa, depending on how dark you like your icing
½–1 c	Whole milk
3⅔ c	Confectioners' sugar

Prep oven and pans: Do not preheat oven. Ensure oven rack is in the center position. Thoroughly grease and flour a Bundt cake pan or any pans you need for your sculpted cake.

Sift flour and cocoa: In a medium bowl, sift together the cake flour and cocoa. Set aside.

Mix wet ingredients: In a large mixing bowl, using a hand mixer, cream the butter and sugar. Continue to beat at medium speed until mixture is pale yellow and fluffy (6–8 minutes). Add the eggs, one at a time, and make sure each egg is completely mixed in before adding the next. Add the vanilla and salt. Mix until combined.

Add dry ingredients: Switch the mixer speed to low. Add half the flour-cocoa mixture, all the heavy cream, and the espresso powder. Mix until ingredients are blended. Add the other half of the flour-cocoa mixture. Mix until fully combined, with no raw flour showing. Bump the speed back up to medium and let the batter mix for 5 minutes, until it's creamy.

Bake cake: Pour the batter slowly into your prepared pan(s) to avoid air bubbles. Set the oven to 350°F. While the oven is heating, place the cake on center rack. Bake for approximately 75 minutes. It's finished when a toothpick inserted in the center comes out clean.

Cool and wrap cake: Once the cake comes out of the oven, allow it to cool for 10–15 minutes, then wrap in plastic wrap. The cake will still be warm when you wrap it—this will help it retain moisture.

(Continued on next page)

Crush espresso beans: Place the chocolate–covered espresso beans in a plastic zip-locking bag. Give them a good whack with a hammer, until each bean is broken. Set aside.

Decide which type of icing you'd like to make: To make a pourable icing that can be drizzled, prepare to add a little extra milk. For a firm cake icing, prepare to use a little less milk.

Make icing: Put a medium saucepan on the stove at medium heat. Add the butter. Stir it every few minutes to keep it from burning as it melts. Once it's melted, stir in the cocoa. Keep stirring until the cocoa is all mixed in. (You can sift the cocoa into the saucepan to minimize lumps.) Add a dash of milk and keep stirring. The icing should be the consistency of soup at this point. Cut the heat down to low and start stirring in your confectioners' sugar. Alternate adding 1–2 cups of sugar with a dash of milk (more if making a pourable icing) and keep stirring until all the confectioners' sugar is incorporated.

Assemble: Arrange cake on a plate or cake board. Use icing to ice the outside. Sprinkle with crushed espresso beans.

Irene's Baking Tips:

- Use superfine sugar, in place of regular sugar.

- Warm the heavy cream in the microwave (warm to the touch, about 1 min) and mix in the espresso powder for easy distribution.

- To bake in a 2-quart domed bowl, prepared with non-stick spray and filled ¾ with cake batter.

- Bake 40–50 minutes, on center rack in oven, until top is firm to the touch or a cake tester inserted in the center comes out clean.

Irene's Decorating Tips:

- Black foam core works perfectly for the top of the hat. It's easy to cut with an X-Acto knife.

- To prevent the foam core from slipping, attach it to the cake by piercing a wooden skewer into the center of the foam, through the cake and into the bottom board.

- Use a coffee grinder to grind the chocolate covered espresso beans. (Warning: The chocolate melts in the center of the blades; carefully wipe off with paper towels . . . who doesn't love chocolate in their coffee anyway?)

- 1 cup of ground chocolate-covered beans is enough.

- Apply the ground beans on the iced cake before icing gets firm and dry.

- To cover the cake with ground espresso beans: first place the grounds on a tray lined with parchment paper; hold the cake with one hand, over the tray; use the other hand to cover the cake with the ground beans. Let the excess fall back onto the tray.

- To place the leftover beans in a container, lift the parchment paper with the beans and fold to create a funnel for easy pour.

CHOCOLATE PRALINE CRUNCH CAKE

EMILY'S HOUSE

This is Rory's cake from the twenty-first birthday party Emily threw for her. The actual cake depicted on the show was covered in chocolate ganache and sparsely dotted with pearls. Since Emily's vision was a cake completely covered in pearls, some serious behind-the-scenes negotiation between Rory and Emily must have taken place in the time between the tasting and the party. Here we've decided to make Emily's version, using white icing. If you prefer Rory's version, simply cover the cake in fudge icing or chocolate ganache instead, and dot it with pearls. If you're really feeling like a Gilmore, use both the white icing and the chocolate. Just save room for a chocolate box!

Pralines:

1 c	Nuts
½ c	Butter
¼ c	Heavy cream
½ c	Sugar
½ c	Brown sugar

Chocolate Cake:

	Butter or shortening, for preparing the pan(s)
	Flour, for preparing the pan(s)
2 c	Sugar
1¾ c	Flour
1½ t	Baking soda
1½ t	Baking powder
1 t	Salt
¾ c	Cocoa, sifted
1¼ c	Coffee, room temperature
1½ T	Vanilla
½ c	Milk
½ c	Canola oil
3	Eggs, room temperature
½ c	Heavy whipping cream
	Pralines, ½ of the batch you made earlier

Make some pralines: Throw the nuts, butter, heavy cream, and both sugars into a saucepan over medium-high heat. Place a candy thermometer in the pan. Use a heat-resistant spatula to stir continuously (and clear the sides of the pan) until the goo is at soft ball stage (234–240°F). Then dump it onto some parchment paper or aluminum foil and let it harden. Once it's completely cooled, whack it with a hammer until the pieces are gravel-sized. Eat a piece (or three), then divide the rest into two piles.

Prep the oven and pans: Preheat oven to 325°F. Grease and flour three 8-inch round cake pans.

Mix the dry ingredients: In a large mixing bowl, add sugar, flour, baking soda, baking powder, salt, and cocoa.

Add wet ingredients: Whisk in coffee, vanilla, milk, and oil. Add three eggs and whisk until just combined.

Make batter and pour into pans: Fold in the cream and pralines. Then divide evenly among your cake pans.

Bake cakes: Bake at 325°F for 26½ minutes (or until top of cakes spring back). Allow to cool for 10–15 minutes. While cakes are still warm, wrap them in plastic wrap. Then allow them to cool completely.

(Continued on next page)

Combine icing ingredients and mix: Add all ingredients (see below) to a large mixing bowl or a stand mixer bowl. Using a hand mixer or stand mixer, mix on low until combined, then turn the mixer up to medium; continue to mix for about 6 minutes. Stop the mixer every 2 minutes or so to scrape down the sides. When it's done, the icing will sound like it's slapping itself.

Separate icing and add pralines: In a medium bowl, add 4 cups of icing (set the rest of the white icing aside). Turn the mixer on low, and add the pralines. Continue to mix until combined. This is your praline-mixed filling.

Assemble the cake: Level the cooled cake layers. Then torte, stack, and ice the layers with your praline-mixed icing. With the smooth white icing, apply a thin crumb layer to the outside of the cake. Chill the cake for 1 hour. Then apply a full layer of the smooth white icing to the outside of the cake. Sprinkle the top with edible pearls (or apply them around the base), decorate with large, real flowers, and serve at a twenty-first birthday.

Icing:

2 lbs	Butter, room temperature
1 lb	Shortening
1 c	Heavy whipping cream, plus a dash more, if needed
4 T	Vanilla
1 t	Almond extract
⅛ t	Salt
1 c	Unsweetened cocoa powder
6 lbs	Confectioners' sugar
	Pralines, the second half of the batch you made earlier

Decorations:

Edible pearls

Large, real flowers for decoration, optional

Irene's Decorating Tips:

- For the icing, to enhance the flavor: Try different extracts or emulsions. I used crème bouquet. It is a favorite and widely used in many bakeries.

- For the filling: Try adding your favorite Swiss meringue recipe to the praline crunch for a wonderful texture.

- To achieve the pearl decoration, I used a silicone mold. Pearl molds can be found either online or at a local hobby store that sells cake decorating supplies.

- Tip for using pearl mold: Lightly dust with cornstarch using a pastry brush or an unused soft makeup brush.

- To release the fondant pearls from the mold: I find it easier by first placing the mold upside down on a flat surface. Use one hand to pry the string of pearls from the mold and hold the end onto the flat surface. Then slowly peel the mold from the fondant string of pearls.

- To create a smooth icing surface, I like to freeze my iced cake and then smooth it with a spatula.

CONVERSION CHARTS

METRIC AND IMPERIAL CONVERSIONS

(These conversions are rounded for convenience)

Ingredient	Cups/Tablespoons/ Teaspoons	Ounces	Grams/Milliliters
Butter	1 cup/ 16 tablespoons/ 2 sticks	8 ounces	230 grams
Cheese, shredded	1 cup	4 ounces	110 grams
Cream cheese	1 tablespoon	0.5 ounce	14.5 grams
Cornstarch	1 tablespoon	0.3 ounce	8 grams
Flour, all-purpose	1 cup/1 tablespoon	4.5 ounces/0.3 ounce	125 grams/8 grams
Flour, whole wheat	1 cup	4 ounces	120 grams
Fruit, dried	1 cup	4 ounces	120 grams
Fruits or veggies, chopped	1 cup	5 to 7 ounces	145 to 200 grams
Fruits or veggies, puréed	1 cup	8.5 ounces	245 grams
Honey, maple syrup, or corn syrup	1 tablespoon	.75 ounce	20 grams
Liquids: cream, milk, water, or juice	1 cup	8 fluid ounces	240 milliliters
Oats	1 cup	5.5 ounces	150 grams
Salt	1 teaspoon	0.2 ounces	6 grams
Spices: cinnamon, cloves, ginger, or nutmeg (ground)	1 teaspoon	0.2 ounce	5 milliliters
Sugar, brown, firmly packed	1 cup	7 ounces	200 grams
Sugar, white	1 cup/1 tablespoon	7 ounces/0.5 ounce	200 grams/12.5 grams
Vanilla extract	1 teaspoon	0.2 ounce	4 grams

OVEN TEMPERATURES

Fahrenheit	Celsius	Gas Mark
225°	110°	¼
250°	120°	½
275°	140°	1
300°	150°	2
325°	160°	3
350°	180°	4
375°	190°	5
400°	200°	6
425°	220°	7
450°	230°	8

RECIPE GUIDE

INDEX